VICTORIAN ESSAYS: A Symposium

Essays
on the Occasion
of the Centennial of
the College of Wooster in Honor
of Emeritus Professor Waldo H. Dunn

VICTORIAN ESSAYS:
A Symposium

EDITED BY

Warren D. Anderson and Thomas D. Clareson

CONTRIBUTORS

Warren D. Anderson Jerome H. Buckley
Thomas D. Clareson A. Dwight Culler
Edgar Johnson Floyd B. Lawrence
David Moldstad Lionel Stevenson

The Kent State University Press

‑

ACKNOWLEDGMENTS

"Symbols of Eternity: The Victorian Escape from Time" is reprinted by permission of the publishers from, Jerome Hamilton Buckley, *The Triumph of Time: A Study of the Victorian Concepts of Time, History, Progress, and Decadence*, Cambridge, Massachusetts, The Belknap Press of Harvard University Press, Copyright 1966, by the President and Fellows of Harvard College.

"Arnold on Etna" is material drawn from various chapters and reprinted by permission of the publishers from, A. Dwight Culler, *Imaginative Reason: The Poetry of Matthew Arnold*, New Haven, Connecticut, Copyright 1966, Yale University Press.

Manufactured in the United States of America
at the Oberlin Printing Company, Oberlin, Ohio
Designed by Merald E. Wrolstad

First Edition

Preface

ON OCTOBER 8 AND 9, 1965, a Conference on Victorian Studies was held at the College of Wooster in honor of Dr. Waldo Hilary Dunn, professor of English from 1907 to 1934. The select bibliography of his writings which follows this preface reveals a lasting concern with the Victorians: his memorable two-volume biography of James Anthony Froude is the latest of a series of distinguished studies covering a half-century of scholarly activity.

Beginning with Dr. Dunn's achievements as biographer and editor, participation in nineteenth-century scholarship at Wooster has remained vigorous. A number of alumni, most of them his students, have made significant contributions to this field: the standard editions of Matthew Arnold's poems, literary note-books, and letters to Arthur Hugh Clough bear President Howard Lowry's name; from Professor Frederick Mulhauser of Pomona has come an edition of Clough's own correspondence. Stanford's Professor John Dodds is the biographer of Thackeray, while at Carleton, Professor Elvan Kintner is bringing out an edition of the letters between Elizabeth Barrett and Robert Browning. Interest in the Victorian period continues among the current faculty at Wooster.

To signalize this tradition and to honor one who has played so important a part in it, a colloquium was planned and invitations extended to four of the foremost active Victorian scholars: Professors Edgar Johnson of the City College of New York, Jerome H. Buckley of Harvard, A. Dwight Culler of Yale, and Lionel Stevenson of Duke. The general plan (given below) of the Conference called for three panel sessions of set papers followed by discussion, and a public lecture, at which Professor Dunn was particularly saluted. This book

[v]

contains the texts of all papers read at the Conference, including that of the lecture.

The essays printed here represent no deliberate prior effort at coordinating themes, yet they prove interrelated to an unexpected degree. As the Conference proceeded, each meeting contributed its own perspective; the resulting combination of unity within diversity is reflected in these pages.

Had it been possible to do so, we should have liked to reproduce here not only the papers themselves but also the spirited exchanges of thought which followed their presentation. As it is, these essays may serve to suggest the scope, the variety, and the involvement of English literature in the nineteenth century, as well as paying tribute to one of its foremost scholars, Professor Waldo Hilary Dunn.

WARREN D. ANDERSON
THOMAS D. CLARESON

Wooster, Ohio
October, 1966

A Select Bibliography
of the Writing of
Waldo Hilary Dunn 1882-

BOOKS

The Vanished Empire. Cincinnati, The Robert Clarke Company, 1904.

The Modern Short-Story (with Lucy Lilian Notestein). New York, The A. S. Barnes Company, 1914.

The Life of Donald G. Mitchell (Ik Marvel). New York, Charles Scribner's Sons, 1922.

Froude and Carlyle. London, New York, Toronto, Longmans, Green and Company, 1930.

Lectures on Three Eminent Victorians (Scripps College Papers No. IV). Claremont (California), Scripps College, 1933.

De Doctrina Christiana (with James Holly Hanford), Volumes 14, 15, 16, and 17 of *The Works of John Milton.* New York, Columbia University Press, 1933-34.

George Washington (with Nathaniel Wright Stevenson). Two volumes. New York, Oxford University Press, 1940.

The Note-Books of Matthew Arnold (with Howard Foster Lowry and Karl Young). London, New York, Toronto, Oxford University Press, 1952.

R. D. Blackmore. London, Robert Hale Limited; New York, Toronto, Longmans, Green and Company, 1956.

Sir Robert Stout (with Ivor L. M. Richardson). Wellington (New Zealand), A. H. and A. W. Reed, 1961.

James Anthony Froude. Two volumes. Oxford, Clarenden Press, 1961, 1963.

ARTICLES CONTRIBUTED TO PERIODICALS

"Thomas Carlyle's Last Letters to James Anthony Froude." London, *The Twentieth Century* (1956), 159: pp. 44-53, 255-63, 591-7; 160: pp. 241-6.

"What Aid Has the English Teacher a Right to Expect from Other Departments?" *Transactions of the Ohio College Association* (1924), pp. 39-42.

"English Composition in Liberal Arts Colleges," *Transactions of the Ohio College Association* (1926), pp. 19-24.

"Richard Doddridge Blackmore," *London Quarterly Review* for January 1926, pp. 44-57.

"Shelley Once More," *London Quarterly Review* for April 1927, pp. 145-53.

"A Microfying Age," *The Holborn Review* (London) for April 1928, pp. 226-31.

"Edmund Blunden and His Poetry," *London Quarterly Review* for July 1928, pp. 74-82.

"Jamie Boswell's Thorn in the Flesh," *South Atlantic Quarterly* for January 1929, pp. 71-82.

"The Centennial of *Sartor Resartus*," *London Quarterly Review* for January 1931, pp. 39-51.

"David Wilson's *Carlyle*," *Sewanee Review* for October-December 1932, pp. 460-75.

"Browning's Second Century" (First Pacific Coast Browning Lecture [7 April 1945]), *Scripps College Bulletin* for July 1945 (Vol. 19, No. 4, pp. 1-28).

"Reflections of a Biographer," *The College Courant* (Journal of the Graduates' Association of the University of Glasgow), Martinmas 1951 (Vol. 4, No. 7, pp. 29-33).

"A Valiant Professorship," *South Atlantic Quarterly* for October 1951, pp. 519-29.

"And We Return," *The Methodist Magazine* (London) for February 1952, pp. 52-54.

Three Poems ("The Flame," "The Presence," "Fulfilment"), *The College Courant* for Whitsun 1952 (Vol. 4, No. 8, p. 111).

"The Wordsworths and the Latter Day Saints," *The College Courant* for Martinmas 1957 (Vol. 10, No. 19, pp. 29-31).

ARTICLES CONTRIBUTED TO *The Encyclopedia Americana*

Elizabeth Gaskell's *Life of Charlotte Brontë*.

John Keble's *The Christian Year*.

Thomas De Quincey's *Autobiographic Sketches*.

The Autobiography of Edward, Lord Herbert of Cherbury.

James Boswell's *Life of Samuel Johnson*.

Samuel Johnson's *Lives of the Poets*.

George Otto Trevelyan's *Life and Letters of Lord Macaulay*.

Robert Southey's *Life of Horatio, Lord Nelson*.

George Du Maurier's *Peter Ibbetson*.

John Gibson Lockhart's *Memoirs of the Life of Sir Walter Scott, Bart.*

Walt Whitman's "Song of Myself."

Richard Doddridge Blackmore.

James Anthony Froude.

Program of the Conference
on Victorian Studies

ADDRESS

Dickens and the Spirit of the Age
Edgar Johnson, City College of New York

PANELS

THE CULTURAL BACKGROUND

Symbols of Eternity: The Victorian Escape from Time
Jerome H. Buckley, Harvard University
George Eliot: A Higher Critical Sensibility
David Moldstad, The College of Wooster

POETRY AND POETICS

Arnold on Etna
A. Dwight Culler, Yale University
Types of the Classical in Arnold, Tennyson, and Browning
Warren Anderson, The College of Wooster

THE NOVEL

The Relativity of Truth in Victorian Fiction
Lionel Stevenson, Duke University
Lyric and Romance: Meredith's Poetic Fiction
Floyd Lawrence, The College of Wooster
Wilkie Collins to Charles Reade: Some Unpublished Letters
Thomas Clareson, The College of Wooster

Contents

VICTORIAN ESSAYS: A Symposium

JEROME H. BUCKLEY

Symbols of Eternity:
The Victorian Escape from Time

EARLY IN HIS CAREER John Stuart Mill remarked that no previous age had been nearly so conscious as his own of the *Zeitgeist*, the spirit of the times, the place of the present generation in the onward rush of history. Confronted on all sides by unprecedented changes throughout their culture, the Victorians felt in a new way the burden of the contemporary, the strange disease of modern life. And much of their large achievement depended upon their will to accept the challenge of the multitudinous present. But with that will commingled the capacity to rise on occasion above time, to view the life of the moment under some aspect of eternity; and the quest for such perspective accordingly became a major theme in Victorian poetry and fiction.

As children by the sea at Yarmouth David Copperfield and little Em'ly naturally assume a world without time and so make "no more provision for growing older, than . . . for growing younger."[1] Miss Havisham of *Great Expectations*, on the other hand, has made a vain, deliberate effort to arrest time; she has stopped the clock in her room at twenty minutes to nine; but the day has worn relentlessly on, the wedding gown has withered on her shrunken body, and the bridal cake has long since mouldered. Aware always of temporal relations and responsibilities, no adult can contrive or decree the release from time that the child habitually enjoys. Yet the desire for transcendence remains, and the dream of eternity may often prove not Miss Havisham's delusion but an enriching vision.

In "The Brushwood Boy," a deeply personal story, Kipling depicted a divided modern sensibility. His hero, George Cottar, a perfectly efficient and apparently well-adjusted English official in India, does his dull duty with great charm and expedition, yet all the while leads a secret dream life far from the routine of his daily work and all the demands of "They" and "Them," the forces alien to his hidden self. Cottar is more fortunate than most dreamers, insofar as he eventually finds a sharer of his dream; on his return to England he meets a woman who for years has likewise imagined the timeless real life as beginning at a brushwood pile on a lonely beach. But many, lacking such fulfillment, have known only the weariness of time, as the pressures of the present closed in upon them.

In the last chapter of his *Biographia Literaria,* Coleridge suggested that some intimation of eternity, gleaned from the perception of a causal nexus between events in human time, alone could make the temporal dimension and man's constant struggle in it seem meaningful. "The sense of Before and After," he wrote, "becomes both intelligible and intellectual when, and *only* when, we contemplate the succession in the relations of Cause and Effect, which, like the two poles of the magnet manifest the being and unity of the one power by relative opposites, and give, as it were, a substratum of permanence, of identity, and therefore of reality, to the shadowy flux of Time. It is Eternity revealing itself in the phenomena of Time: and the perception and acknowledgment of the proportionality and appropriateness of the Present to the Past, prove to the afflicted Soul, that it has not yet been deprived of the sight of God. . . ."[2]

All of the other major Romantic poets, though usually in less abstruse terms, were similarly concerned to discover tokens of permanence or stasis in or behind their passing impressions, and most came to regard their own deepest emotions and intuitions as partaking somehow of the timeless. And the Victorians who followed liked to trust, with Shelley, that the true poet participated in the infinite and the eternal. Arnold indeed insisted, in his preface of 1853, that poetry must treat of great actions, those "which most powerfully appeal to the great primary human affections: to those elementary feelings which subsist permanently in the race, and which are independent of time."[3] Yet he himself as poet was seldom able to achieve such independence. His preface was written to explain the suppression of *Empedocles on Etna,* which like most of his best work was "secondary" and sophisticated, timely and modern, in its sentiments. And Arnold's contemporaries generally were too conscious of the distinctions between past and present to believe that any very wide range of feelings was wholly beyond the touch of time. Coleridge's notion of an eternal substratum differs from most other nineteenth-century literary speculation on permanence in that it has the clearly religious context and significance we find repeatedly in earlier concern with eternity.

According to the traditional time-scheme of Christian orthodoxy, the Past was the period of the world's creation; the Present, the here and now of this mortal life; and the Future, the day of the Second Coming and apocalypse; Eternity entered human time at a precise juncture of history, the death and resurrection of Christ. Such a view seldom appears in Romantic or Victorian poetry, but it receives at least one striking expression, Hopkins' powerful lyric "That Nature is a Heraclitean Fire and of the Comfort of the Resurrection." The "Heraclitean Fire" suggests a possible derivation from Pater's "Conclusion" with its epigraph from Heraclitus and its pervasive fire imagery; and the first movement of the poem captures with incomparable vividness the Paterian sense of flame, flicker, and shifting light, the wonder of "nature's bonfire" constantly refueled, until the argument turns to consider the pathos of man's brief bright "spark," his little life in time:

> O pity and indignation! Manshape, that shone
> Sheer off, disseveral, a star,/death blots black out; nor mark
> Is any of him at all so stark
> But vastness blurs and time/beats level.

Then suddenly remembrance of the Resurrection—a comfort Pater does not consider—"an eternal beam," destroys time, blots out with greater light the "world's wildfire," and

> In a flash, at a trumpet crash,
> I am all at once what Christ is,/since he was what I am, and
> This Jack, joke, poor potsherd,/patch, matchwood, immortal
> diamond
> Is immortal diamond.

In poets less responsive to the appeal of dogmatic theology, the concept of a religious eternity was necessarily less precise. Tennyson's mystical or quasi-mystical experience defied translation into concrete terms; as in his early "Armageddon," so in all his moments of tranced vision,

> All sense of Time
> And Being and Place was swallowed up
> Within a victory of boundless thought.

Browning, despite his devotion to the process of living in the world of sharp sense impressions, could apparently endorse the somewhat bullying abstractions of his Rabbi Ben Ezra,

> Fool! All that is, at all,
> Lasts ever, past recall . . .

or of his Renaissance grammarian,

> What's time? Leave Now for dogs and apes!
> Man has Forever.[4]

And Swinburne could assign an elusive everlastingness, beyond "time-stricken lands," to his vague earth-goddess Hertha. But with the general questioning and inevitable weakening of religious sanctions throughout the nineteenth century, faith in an eternal order became for many more and more precarious, and the idea of eternity, often almost completely secularized, grew correspondingly personal and psychological.

Rossetti, who strove to find a substitute religion in physical love, trusted that the intense sense experience might perhaps grant the lover the nearest possible approach to a conquest of time:

> And shall my sense pierce love,—the last relay
> And ultimate outpost of eternity?[5]

And Arnold, though more tentatively, suggested that in rare moments of reciprocated sympathy between man and woman—"When a beloved hand is laid in ours,"—a man might achieve peace of spirit and even some sense of an eternal dimension:

> And there arrives a lull in the hot race
> Wherein he doth forever chase
> That flying and elusive shadow, rest.

[4]

An air of coolness plays upon his face,
And an unwonted calm pervades his breast.
And then he thinks he knows
The hills where his life rose,
And the sea where it goes.[6]

But in neither poet is there complete certitude; Rossetti asks hopefully whether the sense can actually reach the timeless essence of love, and Arnold allows the lover not precisely to know, but to *think* he knows, the eternity imaged by sea and hills.

Others looked to nature itself, rather than to human passion, for warranty of a permanence beyond time. Wordsworth—to cite the most memorable example—had seen the apparently static subsuming the strongly dynamic in the mountain majesty of the Simplon Pass, where the woods decaying would never be decayed and the blasts of waterfalls were so constant as to seem stationary; and he found in the total harmony "Characters of the great Apocalypse, / The types and symbols of Eternity, / Of first, and last, and midst, and without end."[7] And the young Ruskin shared Wordsworth's response to mountain scenery: "What more, what else," he wondered, "could be asked of seemingly immutable good in this mutable world?"[8] But Wordsworth, especially after his brother John's death by drowning in a storm at sea, learned to suspect nature's benevolence; and Ruskin, haunted by time and change, grew convinced that the "seemingly immutable" was simply fond illusion. As the nineteenth century continued, nature became less and less available as an object of veneration.[9] The Darwinian view of the natural world corroborated Tennyson's description of nature as "red in tooth and claw," and the new scientists, whether biological or geological, would have accepted his picture of the solid hills as flowing from form to form and indeed of all nature as committed to destructive change:

"So careful of the type?" but no,
From scarped cliff and quarried stone
She cries, "A thousand types are gone;
I care for nothing, all shall go."[10]

By the end of the Victorian period, the floral style in the graphic arts, known as the *art nouveau*, might perhaps be construed as a

[5]

highly contrived effort to relate the design of a rapidly moving industrial society to elemental and enduring natural forms. But in literature the motifs from nature that still remained seldom carried connotations of eternity.

"What is eternal, What escapes decay?": the aesthetic Arthur O'Shaughnessy answered the question with a brave will to believe— if all else failed—in art, in "a certain faultless, matchless, deathless line / Curving consummate."[11] Whistler agreed: on a Japanese fan he found all perfect and timeless; the true artist, he said, devoted only to tone and arrangement, had no conceivable interest in things contemporary, the rise or fall, the progress or decadence of his society.[12] Professing a similar creed, the late Victorian literary aesthetes turned for sanction not to Japan but to the theory and practice of the French Parnassians, especially Théophile Gautier, whose "L'Art" Austin Dobson admirably translated:

All passes. ART alone
  Enduring stays to us;
The Bust outlasts the throne,—
  The Coin, Tiberius;

Even the gods must go;
  Only the lofty Rhyme
Not countless years o'erthrow,—
  Not long array of time.

Taking a more realistic view, the aged Tennyson in "Parnassus" denied the perdurability of any rhyme, shaped as all verse must be under the ironic gaze of the "terrible Muses," Astronomy and Geology. Yet even Tennyson would grant that art had greater longevity than most other things short-lived and human; and even if the art work itself were not eternal, it might suggest, as long as it did endure, timeless values and archetypes, images of stasis like his own Sleeping Beauty, "A perfect form in perfect rest." Arnold imagined his scholar-gypsy as immortal because a literary artifact, "exempt from age / And living as thou liv'st on Glanvil's page," and he pictured a hunter on a tapestry in "Tristram and Iseult," forever alert, forever rooted in the greenwood, gazing out at the dead lovers in a bleak chamber.

All such considerations of the power of art to arrest the moment (and they have been frequent in Victorian and modern literature, where one of the main themes of poetry is the nature of poetry itself) recall Keats's superb evocation of the youth and beauty frozen forever on the Gecian urn, the wild ecstasy that will not tire, the leaves that cannot fall. But none repeats the miracle of the ode, which in its ultimate proportion remains, like the urn itself, a silent form able to "tease us out of thought, / As doth eternity."

Though concerned—at least until late in the period—more with the content than the design of art, the Victorians from the beginning were highly self-conscious stylists, deliberately eclectic in their selection of motifs or turns of phrase. Hopkins commended Swinburne for making an effort "at establishing a new standard of poetic diction," but complained that the new language was "essentially archaic" and so ineffective—"now that is a thing that can never last: a perfect style must be of its age."[13] Yet Hopkins himself shaped a new diction at least as rich in archaisms and root meanings as in contemporary idiom. Stylistic eclecticism, though born of a greatly widened response to history, was no doubt intended throughout the nineteenth century to suggest that art was independent of the age and virtually above time altogether. The art work was to be presented "in weird devices," like the enchanted gate of Camelot, with

New things and old co-twisted, as if Time
Were nothing, so inveterately that men
Were giddy gazing there.[14]

But whether or not it could evoke a sense of eternity by style alone, art could clearly seek out a timeless subject matter. Occasionally the poets strove to construct worlds of artifice beyond the reach of change. Morris's *Earthly Paradise*, the longest of such efforts, expressly undertook "to build a shadowy isle of bliss / Midmost the beating of the steely sea." Swinburne's "Forsaken Garden" fancifully depicted a ghostly tract where, all life vegetable and human having already died, death could "deal not again forever," nor change come "till all change end." And Tennyson's "Recollections of the Arabian Nights" conjured up a realm "Apart from place, withholding time," while his "Lotos-Eaters" reproduced the breathless quiet of an unending afternoon in "A land where all things always seemed the same." But Tennyson was too deeply engrossed by the meaning of his own past and the needs of a public present to escape for long into the timeless illusion he could so readily create. And the dominant literary mode of the century—especially in prose fiction, though not without its effect on poetry, too—was a "realism" rooted in the particulars of place and time.

Ruskin, who sought "truth to nature" above all else, asked that the artist, working preferably with his eye on the object, "stay what is fleeting . . . and immortalize the things that have no duration."[15] In other words, intimations of eternity were to be found in the matter of direct experience. Pater developed a similar notion in his essay on Giorgione. "Now it is part of the ideality of the highest sort of dramatic poetry," he wrote, "that it presents us with a kind of profoundly significant and animated instants, a mere gesture, a look, a smile, perhaps—some brief and wholly concrete moment—into which, however, all the motives, all the interests and effects of a long history, have condensed themselves, and which seem to absorb past and future in an intense consciousness of the present."[16] Pater called these heightened moments "exquisite pauses in time"; Wordsworth, more simply, spoke of "spots of time," Joyce, more recondite, of "epiphanies"; all three described what has become a major concern in modern literature.

Stephen Hero defines an epiphany as "a sudden spiritual manifestation, whether in the vulgarity of speech or in a memorable phrase of the mind itself"; and *A Portrait of the Artist* makes it clear that the revelation brings a sense of timeless harmony, "the luminous silent stasis of esthetic pleasure, a spiritual state very like to that cardiac condition which the Italian physiologist Luigi Galvani . . . called the enchantment of the heart."[17] *The Prelude*, as we should expect, links the spot of time to Wordsworth's psychology of memory; the experience reanimates life with purpose, and its remembrance proves an abiding restorative:

There are in our existence spots of time,
That with distinct pre-eminence retain
A renovating virtue, whence—depressed

By false opinion and contentious thought,
Or aught of heavier or more deadly weight,
In trivial occupations, and the round
Of ordinary intercourse—our minds
Are nourished and invisibly repaired.

As an example, Wordsworth recounts an incident recollected from early boyhood, his being separated from his guide in a lonely valley, his flight in terror from an abandoned gibbet, and then his "reascending the bare common" and seeing

A naked pool that lay beneath the hills,
The beacon on the summit, and, more near,
A girl, who bore a pitcher on her head,
And seemed with difficult steps to force her way
Against the blowing wind.

This, he assures us, was quite an "ordinary sight"; yet the whole scene fell suddenly into so sharpened a focus that it was invested forever with a "visionary dreariness" beyond description. Perceiving a unity greater by far than the sum of the separate impressions, the mind thus asserted its rightful place as "lord and master" over "outward sense." In an earlier passage, introducing the description of the Simplon Pass and the sense of eternity its magnificence engendered, the faculty of mind that effects such transformations is explicitly identified as the imagination, and the moment of insight is given the most decisive spiritual significance:

in such strength
Of usurpation, when the light of sense
Goes out, but with a flash that has revealed
The invisible world, doth greatness make abode,
There harbors; whether we be young or old,
Our destiny, our being's heart and home,
Is with infinitude, and only there;
With hope it is, hope that can never die,
Effort, and expectation, and desire,
And something evermore about to be.[18]

Though based on sense perception until the light of sense yields a brighter illumination, the spot of time thus accords with Words-

worth's essentially religious impulse; it seems to fulfill the desire for
everlastingness, for a continuity beyond both sense and time. In the
moment of revelation the physical outline, preternaturally sharpened, wavers, and the object suddenly, like the aged leech-gatherer,
partakes of eternity:

> the whole body of the man did seem
> Like one whom I had met with in a dream;
> Or like a man from some far region sent,
> To give me human strength, by apt admonishment. . . .
>
> In my mind's eye I seemed to see him pace
> About the moors continually,
> Wandering about alone and silently.

Despite its derivation as a term from the Christian calendar, the
Joycean epiphany scarcely goes so far in religious implication. Yet it
represents a modern artist's will to find in the aesthetic perception of
life something of an assurance of value otherwise denied to a secular
age; it offers, at least for the moment, the "silent stasis," the possibility of a fixed and ultimate pattern. Such was the meaning of the spot
of time, with varying degrees of metaphysical association, to many
writers between Wordsworth and Joyce. Rossetti, for example, conceived of the sonnet as "a moment's monument,/Memorial from the
Soul's eternity/To one dead deathless hour," and celebrated in the
form blest moments like the silent noon of shared understanding,
"this winged hour . . . dropped to us from above":

> Oh! clasp we to our hearts, for deathless dower,
> This close-companioned inarticulate hour
> When twofold silence was the song of love.[19]

Meredith presented the moment of insight as a cherished substitute
for a lost eternity; the husband in *Modern Love* remembers an hour
of brief reconciliation when he and his estranged wife, both for once
released from thoughts of their own past and future, caught an image
of selfless, timeless harmony:

> Love, that had robbed us of immortal things,
> This little moment mercifully gave

Where I have seen across the twilight wave
The swan sail with her young beneath her wings.

And Browning, always more intrigued by movement than by stasis,
apparently found spots of time in moments of high aspiration when
the goal was in sight but still unattained; the lover, at any rate, in
"The Last Ride Together" is able to imagine heaven itself as merely
a continuation of the ride, a perpetual extension of his life's unful-
filled mission:

And yet—she has not spoke so long!
What if heaven be that, fair and strong
At life's best, with our eyes upturned
Whither life's flower is first discerned,
    We, fixed so, ever should so abide?
What if we still ride on, we two,
With life forever old yet new,
Changed not in kind but in degree,
The instant made eternity—
And heaven just prove that I and she
    Ride, ride together, forever ride?

In *Marius the Epicurean* Pater offers several instances of what he
must have meant by the exquisite pause in time. Once, when delayed
at an inn, Marius rests in an olive-garden, where he sees far below
him, and as if in a dream, the road he has been traveling and perceives suddenly in "this peculiar and privileged hour" the true direction of his whole life and the possibility of a real world beyond time
"in which the experiences he valued most might find, one by one, an
abiding place." But the most vivid illumination vouchsafed to Marius cannot be so readily translated into abstract metaphysical or moral
terms. It is simply an impression that accompanies the sight of his
friend Cornelius gleaming in golden armor, in an "odd interchange
of light and shade": Marius, sensitive to every detail in the aesthetic
arrangement, feels instantly and apocalyptically "as if he were face to
face, for the first time, with some new knighthood or chivalry, just
then coming into the world."[20] The pause in the garden brings the
sort of revelation that should rightly precede a conversion (like that
of Teufelsdröckh in *Sartor Resartus*), though Marius remains always

too ambivalent to make the final commitment of faith. The vision of Cornelius, on the other hand, is little more than the brief moment that gives added dimension to everyday experience; it is the kind of epiphany we encounter frequently in Victorian and later prose fiction. Mordecai in *Daniel Deronda*—to cite a rather close parallel—beholds Deronda rowing down the Thames toward him, river and rower alike transfigured by the evening light, and feels "in that moment . . . his inner prophecy . . . fulfilled;" Deronda is clearly the ideal young leader he has been looking for, and "Obstacles, incongruities, all melted into the sense of completion with which his soul was flooded by this outward satisfaction of his longing."[21] Similarly Marlow in *Lord Jim*, as he sends Jim off to Patusan, shares with the young man "a moment of real and profound intimacy, unexpected and short-lived, like a glimpse of some everlasting, of some saving truth."[22] To Virginia Woolf, every such moment was a visitation of reality, a sudden unequivocal insight into the heart of life. As everywhere in her own novels, "reality," so understood, is that which "lights up a group in a room or stamps some casual saying, . . . overwhelms one walking home beneath the stars and makes the silent world more real than the world of speech"; indeed, "whatever it touches, it fixes and makes permanent."[23]

Before the nineteenth century, reality was seldom to be defined in such terms. Men long before Wordsworth had, of course, experienced sudden and sometimes soul-shattering revelation. But the spot of time, the private and personal epiphany, took on a new meaning in an age with new concepts of public time, an age with a new awareness of history and obsessive notions of cultural progress and decadence. Troubled by constant change throughout society, by precipitant onward movement often without apparent pattern or direction, the post-Romantic artist might concentrate attention on the qualitative time of the individual and, in doing so, seek to withdraw altogether from the bewildering drift of public affairs. Rossetti is a striking case in point. In his concern with the "moment's monument" that was art, Rossetti grew more and more convinced of "the momentary momentousness and eternal futility of many noisiest questions."[24] John Morley, who was above all the political man, told of meeting him once at the crisis of a general election, and of his declaring a total ignorance of the campaign and remarking that "no doubt one side or the other would get in" and it would make little or no difference which.[25] Later his young protégé Hall Caine was somewhat shocked by his confession: "To speak without sparing myself,—my mind is a childish one, if to be isolated in Art is child's play."[26] Yet not even Rossetti could escape time. Far from being wholly isolated, he was painfully aware of the judgments of his contemporaries; and he suffered—to the point of nervous collapse—the feeling of "being hounded out of society" by Robert Buchanan's *Fleshly School*, an attack which an independent artist should simply have laughed off or ignored.[27] For all his escapist gestures, he was always in large part the product and the victim of the public time he strove to forget.

Rossetti's retreat dramatizes a common and often necessary reaction to a world that was indeed too much with all nineteenth-century men, the world of getting and spending, late and soon, where time was money, the measure of material gain. Yet if the artist could not in fact wholly transcend the age, he could still detach himself long enough and far enough to attempt to see life in some perspective, steadily and whole, beyond what was merely current and timely. And his work could remind men of the quality of the individual life, as well as of its obvious brevity. Cities and Thrones and Powers, as Kipling put it, endured "in Time's eye" scarcely longer than the flower; yet all could learn a salutary truth from the latter, which lived beautifully in the assumption of perpetuity:

This season's Daffodil,
　　She never hears
What change, what chance, what chill,
　　Cut down last year's;
But with bold countenance,
　　And knowledge small,
Esteems her seven days' continuance
　　To be perpetual.[28]

Finally, by examining the intense and privileged moment, art, especially poetry, might suggest that time itself, as man reckons it, was after all man's own invention, a device for dividing eternity into negotiable parts; for

we, thin minds, who creep from thought to thought

Break into "Thens" and "Whens" the Eternal Now—
This double seeming of the single world![29]

If it could restore even briefly a sense of integration, unity and design, art could reduce to harmless illusion the terror of time, the separation of then and when, before and after. Modern man might then return to the all-demanding present with the sustaining perspective of continuity.

[1] *David Copperfield*, Chapter III.

[2] J. Shawcross, ed., *Biographia Literaria*, 2 vols. (Oxford, 1907), II, 207.

[3] R. H. Super, ed., *The Complete Prose Works of Matthew Arnold*, I (Ann Arbor, 1960), p. 4.

[4] Richard A. Altick, among others, argues ingeniously that Browning is satirizing the grammarian and his views of life; but since the idea of eternity occurs frequently, and without irony, elsewhere in Browning, I assume that Browning does indeed feel that "Man has Forever." In any case, see Altick, "'A Grammarian's Funeral': Browning's Praise of Folly?" *Studies in English Literature*, III (1963), 449-60.

[5] Rossetti, "The Dark Glass," *The House of Life*, Sonnet 34.

[6] Arnold, "The Buried Life," lines 91-98.

[7] Wordsworth, *The Prelude*, Book VI, lines 638-40.

[8] Ruskin, *Praeterita*, *Works*, 39 vols. (London, 1903-1912), XXXV, 118. This was Ruskin's response on first seeing Milan in its mountain setting, and the context of the passage makes it clear that the city shares in the glory of the Alps: "Then the drive home in the open carriage through the quiet twilight, up the long streets, and around the base of the Duomo, the smooth pavement under the wheels adding with its silentness to the sense of dream wonder in it all,—the perfect air in absolute calm, the just seen majesty of encompassing Alps, the perfectness—so it seemed to me—and purity, of the sweet, stately, stainless marble against the sky."

[9] The best general treatment of the subject remains Joseph Warren Beach's *The Concept of Nature in Nineteenth Century Poetry* (New York, 1936).

[10] *In Memoriam*, sec. LVI.

[11] Arthur O'Shaughnessy, "The Line of Beauty," *Songs of a Worker* (London, 1881), p. 106.

[12] See J. A. M. Whistler, "Ten O'Clock," *The Gentle Art of Making Enemies* (London, 1890).

[13] C. C. Abbott, ed., *The Correspondence of Gerard Manley Hopkins and Richard Watson Dixon* (New York, 1935), pp. 98-99.

[14] Tennyson, *Idylls of the King*, "Gareth and Lynette," lines 222-24.

[15] Ruskin, *The Stones of Venice*, III, *Works*, XI, 62.

[16] Pater, "The School of Giorgione," *The Renaissance* (New York, n. d.), pp. 123-24.

[17] James Joyce, *Stephen Hero* (Norfolk, Conn., 1963), p. 211; and *A Portrait of the Artist as a Young Man*, ed. Harry Levin, *The Portable James Joyce* (New York, 1947), p. 479.

[18] Wordsworth, *The Prelude*, Book XII, lines 208-15, 249-53, and Book VI, lines 599-608.

[19] Rossetti, "Silent Noon," *The House of Life*, Sonnet 19.

[20] Pater, *Marius the Epicurean*, Chapters X, XII. There are a number of "exquisite pauses" throughout the novel: e.g., the passage describing the snakes (Chapter II), the death of Flavian (VII), Marius's noticing the indifference of Marcus Aurelius to the cruelty of the gladiatorial combat (XIV).

[21] George Eliot, *Daniel Deronda*, Chapter XL. Mordecai later (Chapter XLIII) describes another epiphany, a crucial moment of his youth when on the quay at Trieste, "where the ground I stood on seemed to send forth light, and the shadows had an azure glory as of spirits become visible, I felt myself in the flood of a glorious life, wherein my own small year-counted existence seemed to melt, so that I knew it not: and a great sob arose within me as at the rush of waters that were too strong a bliss."

[22] Conrad, *Lord Jim*, Chapter XXIII. In *The Arrow of Gold* (Part II, Chapter I) the narrator's first sight of Doña Rita brings another and quite Paterian epiphany; and the lady herself, who seems to have in her "something of the women of all time," is strongly reminiscent of Pater's Mona Lisa, in that she is a composite and a quintessence: her face "drew irresistibly your gaze to itself by an indefinable quality of charm beyond all analysis and made you think of remote races, of strange generations, of the faces of women sculptured on immemorial monuments and of those lying unsung in their tombs." The total impression at this exquisite moment is, we are told, one of "absolute harmony."

[23] Virginia Woolf, *A Room of One's Own* (New York, 1929), pp. 191-92.

[24] Rossetti, quoted by Hall Caine, *Recollections of Rossetti* (Boston, 1883), p. 201.

[25] For the anecdote, see Helen Rossetti Angeli, *Dante Gabriel Rossetti, His Friends and Enemies* (London, 1949), p. 254.

[26] Hall Caine, p. 201.

[27] On Rossetti's reaction to Buchanan, see J. A. Cassidy, "Robert Buchanan and the Fleshly Controversy," *PMLA*, LXVII (1952), 65-93, and on his relation to aestheticism, J. H. Buckley, *The Victorian Temper* (Cambridge, Mass., 1951), pp. 161-71.

[28] Kipling, "Cities and Thrones and Powers," *Puck of Pook's Hill* (New York, 1906).

[29] Tennyson, "The Ancient Sage," lines 103-5.

DAVID MOLDSTAD

George Eliot:
A Higher Critical Sensibility

LIOT'S REAL CONTRIBUTION to the English novel
lies in her rational sensibility, that is to say, her rational
awareness of the mental and emotional landscape. More
fully than any novelist before her—perhaps more fully than any
since—she has depicted her characters from a rational perspective
and has represented their inner emotions in rational terms. Eliot
seems to suggest in her fiction the apparent assumption of many
nineteenth century writers on social and political problems, that all
human phenomena can be described by the rational understanding.
Eliot reflects her sensibility in the terms of sense, and her success in
so doing is apparent in the number of critics who have praised her
understanding of her characters' emotional lives.

Arnold Kettle has remarked of Eliot that she "extends the method
of Jane Austen but does not substantially alter it."[1] Perhaps in many
ways the remark is just; but in sensibility Austen and Eliot differ, in
ways revealing of both. Jane Austen's sensibility best expresses itself
in social patterns and gestures. Implied by these patterns is a social
norm of conduct, to which all characters high and low are expected to
measure up. Failure to honor the right social gesture or to act civilly
stamps a character as irrational at that point. For these reasons, Mrs.
Bennet and Mary in *Pride and Prejudice*, are made to seem simply
vulgar and priggish, respectively. But in George Eliot such characters
are many times presented so as to reveal their private inner worlds,
relative to which their actions have reason, even if sophistic reason.
Such presentation may not conceal their stupidity, but it may show
why they choose to be stupid in just those ways. Eliot's sensibility

often operates so as to exploit the sense in a character's rationalization; Austen's sensibility usually operates so as to exploit the nonsense in it.

In this paper I wish to do two things: one, to show the nature of George Eliot's rational sensibility; and, two, to make clear a connection between this sensibility and the kind of thinking Biblical higher critics did. The two points of discussion bear importantly on one another. Eliot was concerned with the total rationale of her characters' lives, not merely with the rationality of their individual acts as judged against some logical scheme. In fact, in *Adam Bede* she directed some sarcastic words at the "misplaced sagacity" of the smugly sophisticated, who thought that "sleek grocers, sponging preachers, and hypocritical jargon" amounted to "an exhaustive analysis of Methodism. . . ."[2] Biblical higher critics assessed Biblical figures with an awareness of the total rationale to be seen in their lives, and usually are likewise suspicious of premature schemes of interpretation. Eliot's awareness of the mental landscape was a matter of perceiving limits, too—limits which her characters did not always see. Here again the higher critics' practice is similar, for they saw Biblical figures as limited by ideas usual to their historical period, their class, condition in life, and so on.

In discussing these matters, we shall first examine passages from Biblical criticisms of Spinoza and Strauss, to suggest their rational, culturally sensitive, and sympathetic attitudes toward Biblical characters. Then we shall consider selections from Eliot's *Adam Bede*, to notice similar attitudes which she displays toward her characters. Eliot sometimes presses these points of view into uses which higher critics themselves did not make, in depicting a character's mind from within. Such readings from *Adam Bede* will, I believe, furnish evidence for suggesting that George Eliot has a higher critical sensibility toward her fictional world. That is to say, Eliot is sensitively aware of historical and cultural limitations of her characters, and is inclined to reflect their mental and emotional landscape within these limits in rational and sympathetic terms.

When higher criticism is mentioned, questions of the authenticity of texts, their authorship, and their relation to each other come to mind. But such questions in Biblical criticism have bred others. World views different from those of later ages (as well as obvious anachronisms) are given rational explanation. At length come efforts to understand Biblical ideas, and even the minds of Biblical protagonists themselves, on their own cultural terms. Moreover, higher critics have explained rationally what has often been rendered in metaphor; and they have viewed the extraordinariness of Biblical figures in the light of their humanity, not of their divinity. Such perspectives, recognizably present in Eliot's novels, are especially to be seen in the writings of Strauss and Spinoza.

Eliot did not acquire these higher critical ways of thinking solely through Strauss and Spinoza, but they did provide her with far fuller rationales for such thinking than she had previously met. Eliot knew certain of their writings well. She had translated all of Strauss's *Life of Jesus* and a good part (perhaps most) of Spinoza's *Tractatus Theologico-Politicus*[3] as well as his *Ethics*. While working with these authors she recorded her general agreement with their conclusions, a judgment she never reversed.

Often when higher critics are mentioned in connection with Eliot, the name of Ludwig Feuerbach is given prominence. In Feuerbach, Eliot found the view that religion can be regarded as the projection of the human mind and its desires. Recent critics have shown how fully she conceived the relations of her characters to each other and sometimes even her narrative patterns themselves in the perspective of Feuerbach. Yet there is a prior and I think quite as important a use which Eliot makes of higher critical thinking come in her awareness of the mental landscape. To this awareness, Feuerbach contributed little that was new. Although he shared many assumptions with Strauss and Spinoza, he was not part of Eliot's frame of reference until the 1850's, approximately five years after she had met Strauss and Spinoza. By that time, her outlook on such matters was largely determined.

Spinoza's *Tractatus Theologico-Politicus*, the translation of which Eliot began but presumably never finished, displays the tolerant understanding toward Biblical figures that Eliot displays toward characters in her fiction. Spinoza emphasizes the importance of the prophets' condition in life and the ideas usual to their times and national group as a key to understanding them.

> . . . Signs were given according to the opinion and capacity of each prophet. . . . And so with revelations perceived through visions. If a prophet was a countryman he saw visions of oxen, cows, and the like; if he was a soldier, he saw generals and armies; if a courtier, a royal throne, and so on. . . . A due consideration of these [prophetic] passage [sic] will clearly show us that God has no particular style in speaking, but, according to the learning and capacity of the prophet, is cultivated, compressed, severe, untutored, prolix, or obscure.[4]

And further, on this same point:

> . . . Nothing is more clear in the Bible than that Joshua, and perhaps also the author who wrote his history, thought that the sun revolves around the earth, and that the earth is fixed, and further that the sun for a certain period remained still. Many, who will not admit any movement in the heavenly bodies, explain away the passage till it seems to mean something quite different. . . . Such quibblers excite my wonder! Are we, forsooth, bound to believe that Joshua the soldier was a learned astronomer?[5]

Prophets were not scientists; rather, they were great moralists and believed in the science of their day.

Vivid imaginations rather than perfect minds were the marks of the prophets, Spinoza said. And he asserts that "If a man abounds in the fruits of the Spirit, charity, joy, peace, long-suffering, kindness, goodness, faith, gentleness, chastity, against which, as Paul says (Gal. 5:22), there is no law, such an one, whether he be taught by reason only or by the Scripture only, has been in very truth taught by God, and is altogether blessed."[6] It is by such criteria that men are judged admirable in Eliot's novels. Their limitations of background or persuasion of mind do not measure them; rather, their charity according to their lights.

Spinoza approaches Biblical narratives reasonably, but he does not press his reason to the point where consistency becomes his end. He opposes the interpretations of Maimonides and other writers, who asserted that no passage in Scripture contradicted any other. Consider his remarks on commentators' efforts to make consistent with each other the appearances of angels to various ancient Hebrews: "Maimonides and others do indeed maintain that these and every other instance of angelic apparitions (*e.g.*, to Manoah and to Abraham offering up Isaac) occurred during sleep, for that no one with his eyes open ever could see an angel, but this is mere nonsense. The sole object of such commentators seems to be to extort from Scripture confirmations of Aristotelian quibbles and their own inventions...."[7] Readers of Eliot can recall in this connection her warnings against "misplaced sagacity." Convinced though she was that "undeviating law" underlay all phenomena, human and nonhuman, the mature Eliot was, like the mature John Stuart Mill, suspicious of premature attempts to systematize human life.

David Friedrich Strauss's *Life of Jesus*, with its rationality of approach, its awareness of cultural and historical factors, and its sympathetic perspective, likewise suggests Eliot's sensibility to her fictional characters. In the course of his argument, Strauss often demonstrated his humane compassionate understanding of the way in which conditions help to shape the individual. In examining Jesus' early education, Strauss carefully notices the possibilities for Jesus' having gained his knowledge. He points out that possibly Jesus met foreign as well as Palestinian Jews, that possibly he was in intercourse with "devout heathens," that he may have met ideas of Alexandrianism and Essenism, and that above all he was indebted to his native spark of genius.[8] Strauss impresses the reader here and elsewhere with his rational yet circumstantial examination of what had often been the province of mystery or metaphor.

Strauss' way of examining the limitations and prepossessions of the gospel writers as a way of comprehending their narratives may be seen in the following passage: "That the Jewish people in the time of Jesus expected miracles from the Messiah is in itself natural, since the Messiah was a second Moses and the greatest of the prophets, and to Moses and the prophets the national legend attributed miracles of all kinds: by later Jewish writings it is rendered probable; by our gospels, certain. When Jesus on one occasion had (without natural means) cured a blind and dumb demoniac, the people were hereby led to ask: *Is not this the Son of David?*"

The idea "that Jesus was the Messiah, would have failed in proof to his contemporaries all the more on account of the common expectation of miraculous events, if that expectation had not been fulfilled by him,"[9] Strauss points out, and he says further that Jesus himself thought in the patterns usual for his age.

> What spectres and doublesighted beings, must Moses and Jesus have been, if they mixed with their cotemporaries [sic] without any real participation in their opinions and weaknesses, their joys and griefs; if, mentally dwelling apart from their age and nation, they conformed to these relations only externally and by accommodation, while, internally and according to their nature, they stood among the foremost ranks of the enlightened in modern times! far more noble were these men, nay, they would then only engage our sympathy and reverence, if in a genuinely human manner, struggling with the limitations and prejudices of their age, they succumbed to them in a hundred secondary matters, and only attained perfect freedom, in relation to the one point by which each was destined to contribute to the advancement of mankind.[10]

Yet with all this discussion urging that Jesus be seen as a man of his age, Strauss goes on to urge (as above) that these limitations do not hinder Jesus' superiority in the matters that count. Strauss speaks of how Jesus penetrates "into the spirit of the law, instead of cleaving to the mere letter, and especially discerns the worthlessness of the rabbinical glosses." Obviously, for Strauss as for George Eliot, a man's immersion in the culture of his time and nation constitutes no barrier to his greatness, though it does determine the terms in which his thinking should be interpreted.[11]

In the rest of this paper, we shall examine Eliot's sensibility to the mental and emotional landscape, as it is revealed in *Adam Bede*. I shall draw largely from this novel, though I believe that Eliot's practice here is representative of her practice in other novels.

Class and condition in life and received ideas of the age all amount to defining limits within which Eliot presents her characters in *Adam*

Bede. Yet for Eliot, greatness is possible within such limits. Those within Plato's cave saw only shadows of reality and were therefore confined by their narrowness of understanding. But for George Eliot, the intellectual and moral landscapes were equally important dimensions. One could be great and unconfined morally though he dwelt in the cave intellectually. Adam Bede himself is so presented, just as Spinoza presents Joshua, perhaps deficient in astronomical knowledge but not therefore less the man.

Adam Bede is the story of Adam's moral coming of age. The novel tells of the "...sad memories, ... warm affection, ... tender fluttering hopes, [which] had their home in this athletic body with the broken finger-nails—in this rough man, who knew no better lyrics that he could find in the Old and New Version and an occasional hymn; who knew the smallest possible amount of profane history; and for whom the motion and shape of the earth, the course of the sun, and the changes of the seasons, lay in the region of mystery just made visible by fragmentary knowledge" (I, 319). Adam's beliefs resulted from his background and times, and in no way indicated weakness of mind. Eliot reflects the higher critics' awareness here: she is sensible of the meaning of Adam's world, in terms of which his life has meaning and even greatness. *Adam Bede* is no "novel without a hero."

Eliot describes the Rev. Mr. Irwine, too, as comprehensible and even admirable, given his background and times. He is "a pluralist at whom the severest church reformer would have found it difficult to look sour," (I, 78), and his personality and outlook are not to be found in a latter-day analysis of the arguments for church reform in the Napoleonic era. Irwine met his world through a "mental palate ...rather pagan, and he found a savouriness in a quotation from Sophocles or Theocritus that was quite absent from any text in Isaiah or Amos. But if you feed your young setter on raw flesh, how can you wonder at its retaining a relish for uncooked partridge in after-life?" Eliot wrote, adding that "Mr Irwine's recollections of young enthusiasm and ambition were all associated with poetry and ethics that lay aloof from the Bible" (I, 100).

That Irwine was inconsistent there is no doubt. Taken in themselves, his grey horse, his dogs, his silver coffeepot all suggested an ease of life hard to reconcile with his supposed profession of selfless clergyman. But Irwine has real kindness, and Eliot urges a broader and more tolerant judgment of him. What Strauss has to say about Moses and Jesus can be interestingly compared to what Eliot says about Adam and—partially—even about Irwine: namely that Moses and Jesus were all the greater for sharing in "the limitations and prejudices of their age," succumbing to them "in a hundred secondary matters" and rising above their age in their moral insight.

The beautiful but shallow dairymaid Hetty Sorrel, whose murder of her child precipitates the main crisis of the book, likewise is shown in terms of the world she knew. But with Hetty (unless you were a man) appearances were not deceiving—individually or as a whole. Hetty had no redeeming inconsistencies, as did Irwine. Her "dreams were all of luxuries [as they might be conceived by a Midlands farm girl in 1799]: . . . white stockings . . . large beautiful earrings, such as were all the fashion . . . Nottingham lace . . . , and something to make her handkerchief smell nice, like Miss Lydia Donnithorne's when she drew it out at church. . . ." (I, 146). Further, Hetty was doubtless foolish in being so impressed by the addresses of a gentleman. Still, "all this happened, you must remember, nearly sixty years ago," Eliot writes, her words echoing Scott's, "and Hetty was quite uneducated—a simple farmer's girl, to whom a gentleman with a white hand was dazzling as an Olympian god" (I, 148). With all these characters, Eliot makes clear the rationale of their lives in the light of their overall patterns. She shows herself aware of the limits of class, culture, and ideas of the age within which and only within which their lives are rationally understandable.

Eliot does not confine her rational and culturally relative perspectives to the world surrounding her characters, however. Employing these perspectives in ways the higher critics did not, she assumes a point of view within the mind and represents the mind as in dialogue with itself. In such passages, the mind never is shown in free association of ideas. Always sentence leads to sentence, with rationally comprehensible connections between them.

The mental world of Hetty Sorrel, over whom Adam and the

young squire fight, is in this way made dismally understandable. The pattern of her rationalizations suggests a whole inner world, a kind of inner culture with limits and ideas peculiar to it, within which Hetty must be understood if her motives are to seem other than arbitrary and mere riddles. Consider in this light the well-known passage where Hetty struts before the mirror in her bedroom (I, 225-26). She put on a black scarf and large earrings. "And she would take out the little earrings she had in her ears—oh, how her aunt had scolded her for having her ears bored!—and put in those large ones: they were but coloured glass and gilding; but if you didn't know what they were made of, they looked just as well as what the ladies wore. . . . Captain Donnithorne couldn't like her to go on doing work. . . . He would want to marry her, and make a lady of her. . . . Marry her quite secretly, as Mr James, the Doctor's assistant, married the Doctor's niece, and nobody ever found it out for a long while after, and then it was of no use to be angry." Hetty can envision herself "the central figure in fine clothes," Eliot goes on; "Captain Donnithorne is very close to her, putting his arm round her, perhaps kissing her, and everybody else is admiring and envying her—especially Mary Burge, whose new print dress looks very contemptible by the side of Hetty's resplendent toilette" (I, 230).

Young Captain Arthur Donnithorne, on whom Hetty's thoughts ran so much, has his mental world revealed too. And he has much to think about, for his illicit affair with Hetty is to produce an illegitimate child. Yet as he stands up before the local farmers at his coming-of-age banquet, his rationalizations show his world as it seems to him. "Did he not deserve what was said of him on the whole?" Arthur asked himself. "If there was something in his conduct that Poyser wouldn't have liked if he had known it, why, no man's conduct will bear too close an inspection; and Poyser was not likely to know it; and, after all, what had he done? Gone a little too far, perhaps, in flirtation, but another man in his place would have acted much worse; and no harm would come—no harm *should* come, for the next time he was alone with Hetty, he would explain to her that she must not think seriously of him or of what had passed" (I, 399). How fully we seem to participate in these worlds of Arthur and

Hetty. Through this inner perspective we look out at the world as it seems to the ignorant dairymaid or the brash young gentleman. And we understand these characters in a way we have never understood any characters in fiction before. Throughout Eliot's novels come these portrayals of the inner state of certain characters, through which the rationales of their actions are made clear. Especially memorable are such representations of Tito Melema in *Romola* and of Casaubon and Bulstrode in *Middlemarch*. In *Adam Bede*, and in other Eliot novels, principal characters are not always revealed in this way. Adam himself is never thus shown to us, and to his detriment. We grasp that he is a powerful character, but we do not understand how it feels to be Adam.

In one sense, the omniscient author convention always had permitted comment on a character's inner life. But in another sense, what Eliot is doing in describing some of her characters is quite new. Her rational sensibility is a trenchant device for conveying this understanding of the world as it appears to limited minds. Eliot abides in her novels by limits far more exacting than those that most omniscient authors observe. Her description of Hetty's or Arthur's inner experience is managed so as to have the experience taken on its own terms, not on the author's. In *Adam Bede*, Eliot's voice is heard often. But she presents these inner experiences in blocks; she does not continually intrude into them in her own voice.

Like Henry James, Eliot offered descriptions of the mind at work, rationalizing, concerned with motives and scruples. James too was concerned with minds prejudiced by cultural patterns. But James's characters are from a narrower stratum of life than Eliot's; his main figures are cosmopolitan or are in the process of becoming so, and *can* comprehend the provincialities which inhibit them even if they do not always do so. Such comparisons throw Eliot's practice into relief. Her rational sensibility usually is set to work on characters limited by class and culture and, by their own nature, unlikely to comprehend their own motives. Often (as with Hetty) Eliot is set to translating irrationalities into rational discourse. She puts into rational focus patterns of behavior seemingly patternless until their cultural relevance is seen. Eliot's representations of her characters' inner reasonings operate to stress these characters' limits, while James's representations often serve to reveal to the characters a sense of their freedom from limits.

George Eliot's novels give one a sense of her breadth of rational awareness. In this quality they remind one that she is of the age of Niebuhr and Mommsen and Strauss, and is critically aware of the tales men have told of themselves, both those with value and those without it. Speaking of her novel *Romola,* her partner in life, G. H. Lewes, once remarked that all George Eliot's fiction was in a sense historical to her,[12] and the remark seems true in a sense perhaps wider than Lewes intended. George Eliot is the first major Victorian novelist to embody in her fiction the idea that other ages and places had to be understood sympathetically and on their own terms if they are to be understood at all. Her rational sensibility, dependent on perspectives like those of higher critics Spinoza and Strauss, has proved a remarkable vehicle for seeing the individual character rationally in respect both to his historical culture and to himself.

---

[1] Arnold Kettle, *An Introduction to the English Novel* (New York, 1960), I, 171.

[2] George Eliot, *Adam Bede* (Edinburgh, William Blackwood and Sons, 1879), I, 52. All subsequent references will be to this edition.

[3] In *The George Eliot Letters,* ed. Gordon S. Haight (New Haven, 1954-5), I, 321, she says (Dec. 4, 1849) that she "could, after a few months, finish the *Tractatus Theologico-Politicus. . . .*"

[4] Benedict de Spinoza, *Tractatus Theologico-Politicus,* trans. R. H. M. Elwes (London, 1900), pp. 29-31.

[5] *Ibid.,* p. 33.

[6] *Ibid.,* p. 80.

[7] *Ibid.,* p. 17.

[8] David Friedrich Strauss, *The Life of Jesus,* trans. from the 4th German ed. by Marian Evans (New York, 1860), I, 208.

[9] *Ibid.,* I, 67.

[10] *Ibid.,* I, 387.

[11] *Ibid.,* I, 301, 266, 363.

[12] *Letters,* III, 420.

EDGAR JOHNSON

Dickens and
the Spirit of the Age

JUST TWO MONTHS past Dickens's twenty-first birthday, when he had been a newspaper reporter for little more than a year, he heard from the gallery of the House of Commons the debate on the Bill for the Suppression of Disturbances in Ireland. Daniel O'Connell, opposing the measure, drew such a harrowing picture of a widow seeking her only son among the peasants slain by soldiers in an anti-tithe riot, that the young reporter could no longer bear it; he put down his pencil, laid his head on his arms and wept.

The incident is both prophetic and symbolic: it catches as in a mirror the essence of Dickens's relationship to the age in which he was to live: his intense concern with the welfare of human beings and the deeply sympathetic emotion that animated him. In a way, Dickens himself is a mirror, reflecting almost all the emergent forces and all the major problems of the Victorian age—not always without distortions and hues of personal feeling, but always in the brightest, sometimes even the most glaring of colors. Though far from an undiscriminating welcomer of everything that was new, he was a warm believer in the characteristically nineteenth-century doctrine of progress and a no less warm supporter of many of its movements for the well-being of men.

To the forces of tradition, as everyone knows, he was hardly so sympathetic. There were ways in which he *was* deeply rooted in the past, more than he was aware of. Those he consciously accepted were concerned with things like quaint, many-gabled houses with twinkling window-panes, plump feather-beds, foaming ale, blazing fires and blazing plum-puddings. Deeper than these were other acceptances in the Christian heritage that he hardly thought about, some that were even hidden from his consciousness. But on the conscious level his attitude toward tradition was almost all a wrathful impatience.

Maintaining tradition, for him, was almost entirely an "obstinate adherence to rubbish," symbolized in that archaic clutter of wooden tallies once used for keeping accounts and still lumbering up the cellars of Westminster until they caught fire and destroyed both Houses of Parliament. In his library at Gad's Hill there were seven fat dummy volumes collectively entitled *The Wisdom of Our Ancestors,* successively subtitled I, Ignorance, II, Superstition, III, The Block, IV, The Stake, V, The Rack, VI, Dirt, and VII, Disease—and one single volume labeled *The Virtues of Our Ancestors,* so narrow that the words had to be printed sideways.

In his novels, his feelings about a hereditary aristocracy are reflected by derisive comments like that in *Bleak House,* that the Dedlock family are as old as the hills and infinitely more respectable; and his feelings concerning the past by details like Mrs. Skewton's gush in *Dombey and Son* about "those darling bygone times...with their delicious fortresses, and their dear old dungeons, and their delightful places of torture . . . and everything that makes life truly charming!" Whenever Dickens went abroad he made almost a cult of visiting dungeons—at Avignon, at Chillon, the underwater cells of the Doge's palace at Venice—and always to burst out with predictable explosions of indignation and horror. Like Goldsmith, he felt, in F. L. Lucas's phrase, that the best thing about the Middle Ages was that they were gone. For Dickens the good old times were the bad old times, and he could not contain his rage at people who colored them with rainbow hues of romance. Their heritage in the present he saw less as the slow conquest and preservation of civilization than as blind and obstructive survivals of barbarism, as tools and instruments of vested interests, privilege, corruption, and injustice.

Correlated with these attitudes were his feelings about progress. He scornfully dismissed those driveling idiots who were distressed by the construction of a railway across the lagoon into Venice. They should thank heaven, he said, that they lived in a time when iron made roads instead of engines for driving screws into the skulls of innocent men. At Rome he was fascinated to see telegraph wires going "like a sunbeam through the cruel old heart of the Coliseum." The pages of *Household Words* and *All the Year Round,* his two successive weekly magazines, are full of enthusiastic articles on scientific advances, new inventions, and industrial processes—and it should be remembered that Dickens kept an iron grip on the editorial policy of his publications and allowed nothing to appear in them that he did not agree with. In his delight with material progress Dickens did not yield to Macaulay or to any Brummagem manufacturer or Manchester cotton miller.

At the same time, Dickens was violently dissatisfied both with the working conditions under which all this new wealth was being produced, and with the meager share of it that seeped down to the laboring classes. From his first appalled glimpse of the Black Country, when he went to Manchester in 1839, he was filled with the furious determination to strike "the heaviest blow in my power" against these evils. Even that sad and sentimental fairy story, *The Old Curiosity Shop,* has one nightmare vision of blazing furnaces, skies black with smoke, and maddened, starving laborers rushing through the satanic streets with flaming brands and frightful cries. Dickens's very next book, *Barnaby Rudge,* boils over in two hundred tumultuous pages describing the Gordon Riots. Almost two decades later still he returned to the theme in the furious attack on the Bastille in *A Tale of Two Cities,* with the shrieks of Foulon as the Paris mob stuff grass into his terrified mouth, trample him beneath their feet, and haul his screaming mangled body up on the rope of a lantern.

Although in such scenes Dickens is giving voice to the horrified fear of revolution that haunted the Victorian imagination, part of their awful power resides in the ambiguous feeling of sympathy and exultation with which Dickens at the same time *identified* himself emotionally with that hideous fury and shared the very rage from which he also shrank back appalled. In these wild pages, if Dickens is in part the respectable and alarmed middle-class householder, he is simultaneously a voice of warning and even of a kind of vengeance, half retribution, half prophecy.

Hard Times represents the fulfillment of Dickens's vow to strike "the heaviest blow in my power" against not merely the workings but the very ethos of the nineteenth-century industrial system. The grim exposure of Coketown was that giant blow: Coketown, with its soot-blackened brick factories like the painted face of a savage, its river purple with evil-smelling waste, its pistons working monotonously up and down like the heads of melancholy mad elephants, its stifling odor of hot oil making a reeking oven of the entire town— and, worst of all, its insistence that life *is* only a hard-facts matter of bargain and sale, from the cradle to the grave—is nothing but the huge jail that the business men and their economic apologists have made of all existence, with the mills and the rows of slum tenements for cells, cut off by black barriers of smoke from even the light of heaven.

Thus far, in the twenty years since he had been a youthful reporter, had the movement of the age brought Dickens. His angry impatience with tradition and the landed aristocracy and his high hopes for a reforming Parliament had flamed into red fury with the merchants and raging disillusion with the politicians poking "the Parliamentary cinder-heap in London." It will be useful to look a bit more closely at the transformation.

Dickens probably heard the last debates on the Reform Bill of 1832, which had its third reading in the House of Commons on March 23rd and passed the House of Lords on June 4th. Of the new Parliament, in which the Whigs outnumbered the Tories three to one, and many of the Whigs were strongly tinged with Benthamite sentiment, Dickens had great expectations. His superior on the *Morning Chronicle*, John Black, its editor, whom Dickens deeply respected, was a close friend of James Mill and a disciple of Jeremy Bentham. John Stuart Mill in his *Autobiography* pays tribute to Black's importance for the advancement of progressive opinion.

Dickens himself was a radical Whig, vigorously supporting the causes of legal, administrative, and political reform and all the humanitarian parts of the radical program. For him, the Tories were those "blue swine," and a "ruthless set of bloody-minded villains," whom he damned heartily. Over a period of a dozen years he was a frequent contributor to *The Examiner*, one of the most influential organs of the utilitarians.

But he grew steadily more antagonistic to the harsher aspects of the utilitarian philosophy, with its Malthusian sentiments about the poor and its Ricardian economics; and he very rapidly revolted against both what it failed to do and the hard-hearted things it did do in Parliament. Though there were some notable achievements—the recasting of municipal institutions, the abolition of Negro slavery, and the first effective factory act—there were also the defeat of Sadler's Ten Hours Bill, the rejection of Lord Ashley's bill to limit the working hours of adults, and—conversely, but worst of all—the passage of the new Poor Law. Humane and generous legislation always proved impossible; oppressive laws passed with the greatest ease.

Dickens attacked the new Poor Law in *Oliver Twist* as a measure of calculated harshness that made the orphanages and the workhouses what the poor had all too great cause to call "Bastilles," where to save the taxpayers' money the indigent, the aged, the sick, and their helpless children were treated as criminals subjected to a prison régime and a starvation diet. It demonstrated to him that to both Parliament and the reformers the pockets of landowners and businessmen still took precedence over the welfare of the people. The accomplishments of the 1830's and the 1840's, not inconsiderable in fact, were paltry in comparison with Dickens's imperious demands, and often evil in their class-bias, their indifference to the needs of the poor, and their penny-pinching cruelty. Political and administrative obstructionism, bribery, and jobbery still strangled all proper public business.

Dickens's ultimate judgment is faithfully echoed by David Copperfield: "Night after night I record predictions that never come to pass, professions that are never fulfilled, explanations that are meant only to mystify. I wallow in words. Britannia, that unfortunate female, is always before me, like a trussed fowl; skewered through and through with office-pens, and bound hand and foot with red tape. I am sufficiently behind the scenes to know the worth of political life. I am quite an Infidel about it, and shall never be converted."

Parliament, in fact, became for Dickens, as it was for Carlyle, a "talk shop," where everything needful for human welfare was obstructed and corrupt bargains were driven behind closed doors. Just as government departments became the Circumlocution Office of *Little Dorrit*, and the machinery of law the fog-obfuscated Court of Chancery in *Bleak House*, the organization of the community a mere matter of buying in the cheapest market and selling in the dearest, and all society one vast jail.

Dickens did not, to be sure, like Carlyle, demand a hero-dictator to sweep the dust-heap away. Instead he terrified respectable middle-class opinion still more, frightened even his friend Miss Coutts, who controlled the Coutts banking fortune, by calling out to workmen to assert the power of their numbers by combining and demanding that the legislature work for human welfare, not for vested interests. And when, a third of a century after the first Reform Bill, the second one of 1867 was passed, he did not share the widespread fears that the floodgates of society were burst open to give power to an ignorant mob. He was confident that the new voters would exercise their electoral responsibilities wisely, he said—and they couldn't be worse, he added grimly, "than the bumptious singers of 'Rule, Britannia,' 'Our dear old Church of England,' and all the rest of it."

Meanwhile as a private individual he himself turned strenuously to working with all his power for innumerable causes of social welfare. Dickens's charitable activities have often been dismissed as if they only paralleled those of Mr Pickwick—the three large tears rolling down the cheek and the hand going to the pocket for half a crown—or those of the Cheeryble brothers, who seemed almost to hope sometimes that a workman's chest would be crushed by a cask of sugar, so that they could get up a donation for him, but who never thought of trying to improve the working conditions that made accidents inevitable. But the parallel is inaccurate. Though, as Mrs Jellyby and Mrs Pardiggle demonstrate, Dickens was scornful of charity that missed the point or represented domineering busy-bodyishness, he was deeply concerned with amelioration and constructive aid.

Here, too, we can see the forces of the age at work in him. Just as he was part utilitarian liberal but part an angry opponent of the utilitarian hard-heartedness represented by such economists as Mc-Culloch and Nassau Senior, so Dickens, who hated many aspects of the Evangelical and Methodist and Nonconformist church movements, toiled in their spirit for many reform activities. We see him in the 1840's enthusiastically aiding the Ragged Schools whose volunteer teachers provided free education to slum children at night, and obtaining financial support for them from Miss Coutts. He could always be counted on to raise money for Mechanics' Institutes, Athenaeums, and Workmen's Libraries, for pension funds for printers and impoverished actors, for free hospitals for both children and adults. He was one of the earliest magazine editors in England to praise the work of Froebel and the first kindergartens.

In *Household Words* and *All the Year Round*, during the 1850's and 1860's, he campaigned furiously and unceasingly for slum improvements—for more light and air, for abundant water supply, for the abolition of the window-tax, for garbage removal, for decent housing in general. In the 1850's he outlined for Miss Coutts an entire scheme of slum clearance, with plans for blocks of working-class flats at low rents, with gas, water, and drainage, public gardens, stores, schools, savings banks, and public libraries. His project resulted in the razing of a slum area in Bethnal Green and the building of the Columbia Square model flats. He worked harmoniously with both those two great evangelicals, Miss Coutts and the Earl of Shaftesbury, in countless tasks of constructive social improvement.

It is interesting to observe the way in which Dickens thus chose the practical application of what seemed to him the essential spirit of Christianity, and bitterly rejected what he felt the intolerance and cruelty of a great deal of Nonconformist and evangelical dogma. He had hated the longwinded Methodist sermons to which he had been subjected in childhood, with their firstlies, secondlies, thirdlies, fourthlies, and lastlies; he abominated the dark Calvinist doctrines of predestination and the gloomy emphasis on damnation. At the very beginning of his literary career he had fiercely attacked sabbatarianism and the endeavor of Sir Andrew Agnew's Sunday Observances Bill to make Sunday a day of horror by closing all the places of resort in which the poor might refresh themselves on the only day of leisure they had in the entire week. The vengeful religion of the Murdstones, of Miss Barbary and the Chadbands, and of Mrs. Clennam praying that her enemies might be consumed with fire and smitten with the plague, filled him with loathing.

He was no less antagonistic, of course, to the Church of Rome, which seemed to him everywhere in Europe a supporter of tyranny and oppression, riveting shackles of superstition on the hearts and minds of the poor whom it professed to succor. He had no more sympathy with the Oxford Movement and the Tractarians, about whom he knew little save that they were concerned with incense, candles, confessions, and a complication of dogma, but whom he was quite clear that he opposed. In religion, therefore, he shared the Methodist feeling that it was a matter of the heart, welling out of loving one's neighbor as oneself, but had no patience with theology or rituals and forms.

We will not deal with Dickens's responses to literature and art. He shows few signs of any influence from the Greek and Latin classics; as Hugh Kingsmill remarks with rough justice, "There is certainly nothing in Dickens's writings to suggest that, whether or not he was put into Vergil, any perceptible amount of Vergil was ever put into him." So, too, of medieval literature. Though in Florence he mused over Dante's bitter exile, the only reference to Dante that I can recall in Dickens's writings is Mr. Sparkler's description of that tragic poet as an eccentric "Old File, who used to put leaves around his head, and sit upon a stool, for some unaccountable purpose, outside the cathedral."

But he knew Elizabethan drama well, not only Shakespeare and Ben Jonson, but many of their fellow dramatists; and from there on Congreve, Sheridan, and all the comic playwrights, down to an almost countless number of nineteenth-century farces, comedies, and serious dramas. He had assimilated the entire range of English prose fiction, from Bunyan and Defoe, through Swift, Fielding, Richardson, Smollett, Sterne, and Goldsmith, to Cooper, Irving, and Scott.

Among his own contemporaries, he welcomed great new talents like Tennyson, Browning, George Eliot, Meredith, Hugo, and Turgenev. Among the French writers of his own time he admired

Chateaubriand, Dumas, Lamartine, and Hugo; he was on terms of intimacy with the leading Parisian dramatists. Thackeray he did not really enjoy, but always spoke of with friendly respect.

He shared Thackeray's complaint that Victorian hypocrisy and respectability would not allow the literary artist to represent men as they really were, while at the same time they sneered that the heroes of English fiction were not as realistic and convincing as those of Balzac and George Sand. "O my smooth friend," he exclaimed, "what a shining impostor you must think yourself, and what an ass you must think me, when we both know perfectly well that this same unnatural hero must be presented to you in that unnatural aspect by reason of your morality, and is not to have, I will not say any of the indecencies you like, but not even any of the experiences, trials, perplexities, and confusions inseparable from the making or unmaking of all men!"

Dickens recognized the superiority of painters like Ingres, Degas, Manet, and Courbet at the International Exhibition of 1856 to most of his English artist friends—men like Egg, Ward, Stanfield, and Frith; and if at first he greeted the Pre-Raphaelites with philistine scorn and wrote a contemptuous article about Millais's *Christ in the Carpenter's Shop*, he later came to see the power of their art and became an admiring friend of both Millais and Holman Hunt.

His interest in science, again like that of many of his contemporaries, focused predominantly on its practical applications. The pages of his two successive magazines are full of articles on scientific inventions in technology, agriculture, and industrial machinery, but an appreciable number also deal with scientific theory. Faraday's lectures on chemistry and physics inspired an entire series of articles in *Household Words*.

Darwin's *Origin of Species*, which startled so many dovecotes in nineteenth-century thought, was greeted in *All the Year Round* with an article of respectful and lucid exposition which called attention to the far-reaching implications of its theory. The "dreadful hammers" of the geologists clinking away at "every cadence of the Bible phrases," that so distressed poor Ruskin, had no terrors for Dickens. He read Lyell's *Antiquity of Man* with calm acceptance; and the excited controversy about Bishop Colenso's demonstration that the Pentateuch and the Book of Joshua could not be considered reliable historical documents seemed to him so much obscurantist superstition.

All told, far from justifying Dean Inge's remark that "the number of great subjects in which Dickens took no interest whatsoever is amazing," or Bernard Shaw's claim that he was unaware of the cultural upheavals of the age, Dickens seems to me at least as responsive to their manifestations in art, literature, and science as almost any of the other great writers of his time.

I must now pass on to the closing stages of Dickens's career. In them, I think, Dickens becomes even more deeply sensitive to the deepest forces at work in society. Every reader today can see these developments being foreshadowed in the pervasive fog-imagery of *Bleak House*, with its assault on vested interests and institutions, archaic traditions, and greed fettering generous action and beclouding vision; and in the no less pervasive jail-imagery of *Little Dorrit*, with its sense of an imprisoning system constraining men's very minds; in *Hard Times* and its onslaught on a laissez-faire philosophy of material acquisition that really believes in freedom only for pitiless rapacity. It is strange to note that some of Dickens's contemporaries who should have sympathized, one would have thought, with his sentiments, more often recoiled. Macaulay, who had bravely fought Negro slavery, could see only what he dismissed as "sullen socialism" in Dickens's attack on wage slavery; and John Stuart Mill, the heir of Bentham's war against legal obstructionism, did not welcome the Dickens of *Bleak House* as a fellow warrior, but only saw and resented Mrs Jellyby and Mrs Pardiggle as what he called a vulgar sneer at the rights of women.

But Dickens's divination was to pierce deeper. To share fully in its probing gaze we must retrace our steps part of the way. Dickens first visited the United States in 1842, feeling himself a convinced and ardent democrat who would understand the great country that had grown up in the shelter of the tree of liberty. He expected to write a book in which its shining image would counteract the old-world prejudices of such previous British observers as Captain Basil Hall, Mrs Trollope, and Harriet Martineau. What he actually wrote about America, in *Martin Chuzzlewit* and *American Notes*, turned into something far different from the eulogy he had intended.

Now Dickens's criticism of American society has often been angrily dismissed as superficial and distorted—and in certain of its more obvious targets, such as spittle, tobacco juice, a boorish and intrusive lionization, and the corrupt vulgarity of the American press, there is no doubt an element both of superficiality and of caricature. His disillusion, however, was rooted in something far more profound than mobbing, mendacity, and bad manners.

What disturbed—it would not be an exaggeration to say what frightened—Dickens in America was a sort of anonymity in the bulk of its population, an absence of true individuality and personality, despite all the loud and even freakish assertion of independence —nothing less than a disappearance, an emptiness of the self. (Of course I don't mean that he found no individuality in Longfellow, Washington Irving, Cornelius Felton, George Bancroft, W. H. Prescott, George Ticknor, and scores of other Americans who became warm friends; I am talking of a mass phenomenon.) It was more than uniformity, more even than conformity; it was as if behind all these grotesquely varied masks there were nothing but hordes of hollow men—in T. S. Eliot's phrase—noisily asserting a void.

Though Dickens probably did not know, Tocqueville only a few years before in *Democracy in America* had observed that a mass-production society tended to create mechanical men devoid of any true core of personality. Sixty years later, in *The American Scene*, Henry James was to complain on returning to America of "the monotonous commonness"—that is, the sameness—of American character and the tediousness of its social life. Sinclair Lewis documented the charge in *Main Street* and *Babbitt*.

In *Martin Chuzzlewit* this perception emerges in a sort of inverted Kafkaesque surrealism, in which all the crowds of people, instead of feeling, like Kafka's characters, a nameless and unidentifiable sense of guilt—which would at least be human—are always shouting loud and violent challenges to nonexistent opponents. There is the

Watertoast Association of United Sympathizers, whose sympathies or reasons for sympathizing it is impossible to discover. There is the famous "Pogram Defiance" of unknown enemies who are not even aware of Elijah Pogram's existence, or rather of his nonexistence, for he is a stuffed man asserting no more than a diffused bellicosity in support of nothing except an ego without any reality. For all their surface variety in oddity, these people are all alike. Jefferson Brick, Colonel Diver, Major Pawkins, General Choke, Lafayette Kettle, Professor Ginery Dunkel, Mrs Hominy, the Two Literary Ladies, Zephaniah Scadder, Hannibal Chollop, are really all the same non-human beings. They represent the abolition of man, the emergence of the faceless faces.

But they were also—Dickens was to find the conviction creeping upon him in the course of the next two decades—the wave of the future. And in *Our Mutual Friend* the future has arrived. "The Voice of Society," as Dickens ironically calls his hideous perversion of a Greek chorus in that novel, voicing the judgments of conventional respectability, is merely the faceless men in British garb. They now dominate the world far more absolutely than Sir Leicester Dedlock ever dreamed of ruling it. Podsnap, Buffer, Boots, Brewer, Fascination Fledgby, the Lammles, Lady Tippins, the Veneerings, Lord Snigsworth "snorting at a Corinthian column with . . . a heavy curtain going to tumble down on his head"—these are really the masters of nineteenth-century society as Dickens has at last come to see it. Like their American forerunners in *Martin Chuzzlewit*, they all "did the same things; said the same things; judged all subjects by, and reduced all subjects to, the same standard"—the standard of a vulgar, barbarous, monetary idolatry disguising itself as civilization. All of which Dickens symbolizes in turn by the image of the dust-heaps, those huge mountains of filth and ordure representing wealth which is now the solitary, respectable, dominant, non-human goal.

The identity is perfectly clear in parallel passages from the two books. "Whatever the chance contributions that fell into the slow cauldron of their talk," young Martin Chuzzlewit observes, "they made the gruel thick and slab with dollars. Men were weighed by their dollars, measures gauged by their dollars; life was auctioneered, appraised, put up, and knocked down for its dollars." Now *Our Mutual Friend*: "A man may do anything lawful for money," says the genius at promotion, "but for no money!—" "Have no antecedents, no established character, no cultivation, no ideas, no manners; have Shares. Where does he come from? Shares. What squeezes him into Parliament: Shares. . . . Sufficient answer to all; Shares. O mighty Shares! To set those blaring images so high, and cause us smaller vermin, as under the influence of henbane or opium, to cry out night and day, 'Relieve us of our money, scatter it for us, buy us and sell us, ruin us, only we beseech ye, take rank among the powers of the earth, and fatten on us!'"

It is interesting, let us here note as a curiosity, to see how Dickens's analysis in *Our Mutual Friend* anticipates a famous one which Matthew Arnold was to make a few years later in *Culture and Anarchy*. For plainly Podsnap and all of his circle representing "The Voice of Society" are the group Arnold calls philistines, the dominant, destructive, major power in nineteenth-century society. Dickens's wit of course, is not the elegant, wire-drawn wit of Arnold; it has the cutting edge of a meat ax, but it cuts the same way. Mr. Podsnap's notions of the arts, for example:

"Literature: descriptions of getting up in the morning at eight, shaving close at quarter past, breakfasting at nine, going to the City at ten, coming home at half past five, and dining at seven; Painting and Sculpture: models and portraits representing professors of getting up in the morning at eight, shaving close at quarter past, breakfasting at nine, going to the City at ten, coming home at half past five, and dining at seven; Music: a respectable performance (without variations) on . . . wind instruments, sedately expressive of getting up in the morning at eight, shaving close at quarter past, breakfasting at nine, going to the City at ten, coming home at half past five, and dining at seven. Nothing else to be permitted to those same vagrants, the Arts, on pain of excommunication, Nothing else To Be—anywhere!"

The barbarians of Arnold's analysis are represented in *Our Mutual Friend* by Eugene Wrayburn and Mortimer Lightwood, those two weary aristocrats who believe in nothing, and accept invitations from the philistines because it is easier than writing a refusal. The populace are all the victims of the book—Betty Higden, Sloppy, that poor little clerical wage slave, R. Wilfer; Bella's helpless father, Mr. and Mrs. Boffin, Gaffer Hexam, his daughter Lizzie, Rogue Riderhood, Jenny Wren, the crippled dolls' dressmaker, the patriarchal and exploited Jew, Mr. Riah. Dickens even dramatizes Arnold's point that some of the *worst* of the populace, seeking to raise themselves in the world, become infected with the life-destroying standards of the philistines. This is shown in Bradley Headstone, the schoolmaster, and his pupil, Charley Hexam, who grows meaner and nastier as he acquires an education and takes "The Voice of Society" as his guide.

Matthew Arnold, to be sure, might have been somewhat startled at first to think of fat, trotting, illiterate Mr. Boffin as an apostle of culture. There is little enough that Noddy Boffin knows of "the best that has been thought and spoken," and little that on the intellectual level he understands of "the study of perfection." But surely in his own intuitive way of feeling, springing from the heart, Mr. Boffin represents sweetness and light, and is seeking as he dramatizes for Bella Wilfer the errors of her judgments and action "to make reason and the will of God prevail." Just as his creator, Dickens, is doing—both with her and with the aristocrat-barbarian Eugene Wrayburn, as he subjects him to a baptismal immersion by near-drowning, the death of his old selfish levity, and a spiritual rebirth. In the end, the novelist who had pasted labels on blacking bottles in his childhood, and the scholarly poet-critic steeped in classical learning, have converged to judge their age by like if not identical standards, to condemn its evils with equal sharpness, and to uphold kindred ideals of conduct.

Our Mutual Friend was Dickens's last completed novel. Yet even this incomplete and truncated survey of some of his themes—and it could be expanded into an entire book—will serve to reveal how fully he responded to and reflected that serious awareness of the major forces of his age, that earnest concern with its problems, that burning concentration upon its crucial issues, which is what we mean when we speak of a writer reflecting the spirit of the age.

There are some austere historians who stiffen into a puritanical disapproval when we seek in imaginative writers for valid knowledge about the past, and who rigidly insist on confining the search to what they regard as more scientific factual evidence. I have heard Mr. J. H. Plumb, for example, contend that he knows no writer more unreliable than Dickens as a source of factual information about the nineteenth century. Lord Chief Justice Denman or the Vice-Chancellor whom Dickens quotes in his preface to *Bleak House* would undoubtedly have agreed with Mr. Plumb. Lord Denman derided Dickens's onslaught upon the legal system as "belated and now unnecessary," and the Vice-Chancellor argued that any slight leisureliness in the pace of the Court of Chancery was all the fault of a stingy public which refused to provide salaries for a larger number of judges.

But Dickens thought this a wild legal joke that must have originated with Conversation Kenge or Mr. Vholes, and I am inclined to agree with him. In 1844 he had brought a Chancery suit against a crew of piratical publishers who had flagrantly plagiarized *A Christmas Carol*; in spite of winning every legal point under dispute Dickens not only received not a penny in damages but found himself saddled with court costs of £700. Under these circumstances he seems to me not unjustified in feeling that courts of law did not always mete out justice. The case of Jarndyce and Jarndyce, in *Bleak House*, was based on the notorious Jennings case, involving the disputed property of an old miser of Acton who had died intestate in 1798, leaving almost £1,500,000. When one of the claimants to the estate died *in 1915* (forty-five years after Dickens himself was dead) the case was still unsettled and the court costs amounted to £250,000. There thus appears to be some slight foundation for Dickens's conclusion that legal processes were sometimes rather slow and rather expensive.

But we must not, on the other hand, be carried away into regarding everything that a novelist writes as veridical evidence about the life of his age. There is indeed danger if we use him uncritically to establish whether or not some specific event took place at a given time. He may be simply wrong, or unconcerned about the facts, or deliberately distorting. He may in a lapse of memory or even in sheer ignorance depict ladies as wearing crinolines ten years before they came into fashion, or, for dramatic purposes, fuse together as occurring at the same time things that really took place at widely separated periods. Again, as Dickens did in *Barnaby Rudge*, he may be using the Gordon Riots of 1780 to comment on the industrial strikes and Chartist disorders of the 1840's, counting on his readers to perceive certain parallels and resemblances that are not complete but that are meaningful. Still again, as Dickens to some degree did, he may be writing fantasy disguised as sober reality—a technique that Franz Kafka pushed still further in such novels as *The Castle* and *The Trial*—though fantasy vibrant with deep implications not only about the social dilemmas of his time, but about the insoluble problems of man's condition in the world and man's fate. There is no substitution for insight in the interpretation of our evidence.

The same caution, for that matter, must be brought to the use of "factual" documents. The man who produced them may have been mistaken, uninformed, faulty in memory, prejudiced in judgment, stupid or superficial, or even plain lying. Unless we allow for the political bias behind the lively *chronique scandaleuse* of Thomas Creevey, we may be seriously misled by his ragings at the perfidy and "infinite meanness" of the Tory George Canning or his delighted account of the tricks and stratagems of "Old Wickedshifts," Lord Brougham. So that here too, without judgment, our sources may be a smoke screen rather than an illumination.

When we are dealing with cultural history, with the ebb and flow of ideas, the feelings and beliefs that were animating men's minds and hearts, the problems of the times—in a word, with the spirit of the age—there are no witnesses ultimately *more* significant than the storytellers and poets. Among them no writer of Victorian England reflects the complexities of his era more richly, copiously, sensitively, variedly, and completely than Charles Dickens.

A. DWIGHT CULLER

Arnold and Etna

THE SUBJECT OF THIS ESSAY is a brief period in the life of Matthew Arnold which I take to be the most important spiritual crisis of his entire life. As such, it is widely reflected in his poetry. The time I have in mind is the period September 24-27, 1849, when Arnold took a three- or four-day walking tour up into the Bernese Alps. He had been staying in the Hotel Bellevue in Thun, Switzerland, where, the previous September, he had met a small French girl whom we have come to know as Marguerite. Now he was back to see her again, and he was, as he wrote to Clough, "in a curious and not altogether comfortable state."[1] Doubtless he realized that something would have to be decided about their relation, either that it would go forward or that it would not; and he was also upset about the political situation. Just the year before, 1848, he and Clough had lived through the days of revolution, and the net effect upon Arnold had been to accentuate his tendency toward withdrawal. Writing to Clough in November 1848, he said, "I . . . took up Obermann, and refuged myself with him in his forest against your Zeit Geist." "Better that, than be sucked for an hour even into the Time Stream in which they and [you] plunge and bellow."[2] Obermann was the eponymous hero of a novel by the French author, Etienne Pivert de Sénancour. Arnold had encountered him in 1847 and had made him "the master of my wandering youth."[3] So much so that he decided to embody his gloomy spirit in a drama on the subject of Lucretius. Ultimately, however, he took Empedocles as his subject, doubtless because his life, and especially his suicide in a fiery volcano, provided a better symbol of what he wanted to say than Lucretius' death by a love-potion. Thus, in the summer of 1849 he was at work upon this, and J. C. Shairp wrote to Clough, "I saw the said hero—

Matt—the day I left London. He goes in Autumn to the Tyrol with Slade. He was working on an 'Empedocles'—which seemed to be not much about the man who leapt in the crater—but his name & outward circumstances are used for the drapery of his own thoughts."[4] How much they were so used Shairp would have realized if he could have followed Arnold to Switzerland (his actual destination rather than the Tyrol) and seen him act out his own drama in the Bernese Alps.

But first we must return to Marguerite. The poems about her are embodied largely in the series *Switzerland*, and the thing to realize about these poems is that they are *not* love poems. Rather they are un-love poems. They are poems about the process of falling out of love, of putting love, and especially passion, behind one. The most dramatic and revealing of the group is *Parting*, in which Marguerite is seen descending the stair and her voice is so liquid and lovely that she seems the very epitome of the fresh and spring-like beauty of the world. Gradually, however, as she comes nearer, and the poet's attention shifts from her voice to her figure, then to her face and lips— "Sweet lips," he says, "this way!" But then—and it must be admitted that the effect upon a modern reader is a little comic—he starts back with the cry,

> To the lips, ah! of others
> Those lips have been prest,
> And others, ere I was,
> Were strain'd to that breast.

So saying, he flings off up the mountain to take refuge in the arms of Mother Nature.

> Blow, ye winds! lift me with you!
> I come to the wild.
> Fold closely, O Nature!
> Thine arms round thy child.

What Marguerite had done to deserve this treatment we do not know. In a poem written ten years later, while Arnold was revisiting Switzerland with his wife, he speculates on what had happened to her in the interval, and one of his suggestions is that she has wandered back to France and become a prostitute, as people like her too easily do. This suggestion has earned for Arnold a great many hard words among the critics, who say that the thought is unworthy of him. Perhaps it is, but the real trouble is that the critics have so fallen in love with Marguerite that they cannot endure the process of separation which is the main theme of the poem. In many of Arnold's works he is concerned with probing through the fair exterior of the world to the harsh reality which lies beneath. We know from several of his letters that he seems at this time to have been discovering underneath the illusion of Romantic love the fact of sex, and apparently this fact is one element in his disillusionment with Marguerite.

But even without that element it is apparent that Arnold was discovering that Marguerite was not the person he had imagined her to be. Initially, she is presented as a joyous, spring-like beauty. But as the poems proceed, she appears rather to vacillate between two roles —that of a restless, passionate intensity and a light, mocking frivolity—and the reader is aware that these are the roles that Arnold has been playing too. In his earlier poetry Arnold has had two ways of meeting the world's evil—one by mockery, by assuming the mask of indifference, and the other by defiance, by raging against the gods. The latter is the more primitive and, as Arnold puts it in poems like *A Summer Night*, is one of two alternatives, either to be a Madman, defying one's destiny, or to be a Slave, knuckling under and submitting. There is also, of course, the Divided Soul—Dipsychus in Clough's phrase—who cannot decide what he should be and alternates helplessly between them. More sophisticated than these is the Reveller, or, more precisely, since he revels with but half his mind, the Strayed Reveller, the man who remains detached from it all through a light and airy mockery; and this is the role that Arnold has most consistently played. But now he discovers to his chagrin that Marguerite can play it too. "Light flows our war of mocking words," he says, and he is annoyed that they cannot speak openly with one another. He knows that other men conceal their thoughts for fear of indifference or ridicule, but he did not think that lovers did so, and he expresses this thought in *The Buried Life*.

It is in this poem, written almost certainly during this period, that

Arnold develops his theory of the Buried Life. The theory says that although on the surface we live partial and fragmented lives, assuming guises and roles that are not really ours, far beneath the surface flows the stream of our True or Buried Self. Occasionally we become conscious of this stream, and when we do, our desire is to bring it to the surface, and unite it with our other streams, so that we can flow on, clear and strong, directly toward the sea. It seems very significant that Arnold should have developed this theory in connection with a love poem, for it is in love, and especially the love leading to marriage, that you need to know who and what you are. In poetry you do not. Poetry even encourages the playing of roles, in adopting this or that form of life not because it is your own but so you can enter into and understand it. But in marriage you have to be one single person, and in the happy marriage you have to be the right person. You are looking, says Arnold, for "the twin soul which halves [your] own,"[5] and this means that you need to know, not merely the twin soul but also your own. You need to decide whether you are a Madman or a Slave, a Strayed Reveller or Dipsychus, or not any one of these at all but something quite different. Arnold was constrained to make this decision between September 24-27, 1849.

In the poem *Parting* Arnold represents himself as fleeing from Marguerite up into the mountains, and in a letter to Clough dated September 23 he quotes a few lines from this poem—

I come, O ye mountains—
Ye torrents, I come,

and then adds, "Yes, I come, but in three or four days I shall be back here, and then I must try how soon I can ferociously turn towards England."[6] The story of what happened in those three or four days is told in a poem which is not part of the *Switzerland* series but which ought to be read in between *Parting* and the next poem, *A Farewell*. It is called *Stanzas in Memory of the Author of 'Obermann.'* It is dated by Arnold November 1849, but that evidently refers to the time when it was completed, for Arnold says that it was "conceived, and partly composed, in the valley going down from the foot of the Gemmi Pass towards the Rhone."[7] This was country that Arnold had

visited the previous September, and in revisiting it now he was re-
newing associations with two Romantic solitaries, Byron and Obermann. Byron had traveled that way in 1816, and his impressions of
the place, as recorded in his journal, were spread at large over the
pages of John Murray's *Handbook to Switzerland*, which Arnold
carried with him. Byron had even gone to Thun, and one may be
sure that if there was a predecessor of Marguerite in the town, he had
fallen in love with her. Arnold was uncomfortably aware that his
travels in Switzerland, his falling in love, and his writing poetry
about it were all reminiscent of Byron. Hence his remark in 1848
that the "whole locality is spoiled by the omnipresence there of that
furiously flaring bethiefed rushlight, the vulgar Byron."[8]

Obermann was both better and worse. He had an austerity and
gravity that Byron lacked, but he also lacked Byron's force. George
Sand, analyzing him in relation to other varieties of Romantic melancholy, says that he represents the clear consciousness of incomplete faculties. "René signifies genius without will; Obermann moral
elevation without genius. . . . René says, 'If I could will, I could do
it.' Obermann says, 'Why bother willing; I never could do it.' "[9] In
Sand's view he was the patron saint of impotence, and his gravity was
the gravity of death.

Nevertheless, it was to this writer that Arnold had attached himself in 1847, and now, as he revisits the country around Lake Ge-
neva, he tries to explain why. Essentially, his explanation is that
Obermann alone looks fixedly and steadily on "the hopeless tangle
of our age." Hence, he is a better spiritual guide than either Wordsworth, who averts his gaze from half of human life, or Goethe, who
lived in a less tumultuous time. "To thee we come, then!" cries the
poet, and in this remark he dramatizes his election of Obermann two
years before as "the master of my wandering youth." But then, as he
considers the matter more deeply, he cries, "—Away!"

Away the dreams that but deceive
And thou, sad guide, adieu!
I go, fate drives me; but I leave
Half of my life with you.

"I in the world must live," says the poet, and he ends the poem by bidding to Obermann "a last, a last farewell!" Arnold calls the poem *Stanzas in Memory of the Author of 'Obermann,'* but it might almost better be called *Stanzas in Repudiation of the Author of 'Obermann,'* for this is what actually happens in the poem. "My separation of myself, finally from him and his influence," wrote Arnold to a friend, "is related in a poem in my Second Series."[10]

I have said that this moment of communion on the mountain represents the most important spiritual crisis in Arnold's entire life because in rejecting Obermann, Arnold was putting behind him all the turbulence and unrest, the *Sturm und Drang,* that had plagued him in previous years. And in saying, "I in the world must live," he was clearly foreshadowing his future career as an Inspector of Schools, a literary and social critic. He was also, of course, making his decision about Marguerite, for she represented the same spiritual morbidity as did Obermann. There can hardly be any doubt, then, that when Arnold went back down to Thun, to see "how soon I can ferociously turn towards England," he found his task much easier than if he had not written the *Stanzas in Memory of the Author of 'Obermann'* in the mountains.

To free himself from Obermann, however, was only half the task. Arnold had also to discover who he properly was, and this he did in the final stanza of the poem. For when he said, "I in the world must live," he did not mean that he was to be a Slave. Rather he meant that he was to be one of a new group of characters who here enter his poetry for the first time and whom he calls "The Children of the Second Birth, / Whom the world could not tame." The phrase comes from the Gospel according to St. John, where it is said, "Except a man be born again, he cannot see the kingdom of God." Arnold alludes to this passage in his letter of September 23, where he tells Clough, "Marvel not that I say unto you, ye must be born again," and he then goes on to declare that Clough is almost the only living one he knows of "The children of the second birth / Whom the world could not tame."[11] But although Clough is almost the only living example of this group, there is a "small transfigured band" of them among the dead. Arnold's list—"Christian and pagan, king and slave"—suggests that Thomas à Kempis, Marcus Aurelius, and

Epictetus would be among the group, but so too, he now perceives, is Obermann. For the deeper message of Obermann is that it does not matter whether one lives in the world or out of it, so long as he remains "unspotted by the world." Thus, by rejecting a surface conception of Obermann for a more profound one, Arnold has rejected the surface conception of himself for his True or Buried Life.

He immediately applied this discovery to his relation with Marguerite, for in the very next poem of the series, a *Farewell*, he informs his beloved that they but "school [their] manners, act [their] parts" in pretending to be strong Byronic lovers. Actually, the true bent of both their hearts is to be "gentle, tranquil, true." Unfortunately, Marguerite has not yet made the discovery about her self that Arnold has made about his, and therefore they must part. Not all the poems in the series are consonant with this interpretation, but the general tenor of the group is that the lovers are kept apart not by external circumstance but by inner resistance. The God that had warned him back was the god of his own nature, and the twin soul that halves his own was not Marguerite but Frances Lucy Wightman. To her, the mild and gentle daughter of an English judge, was addressed that milder and gentler series of poems, *Faded Leaves.*

Unfortunately, Arnold was already engaged upon his drama *Empedocles on Etna*, which is the very essence of all that he had put behind him. We have already noticed that Shairp felt that Arnold was merely using the philosopher as a cloak for his own thoughts and feelings, and this view is strengthened when we see Arnold writing, on the very day before he ascended the Bernese Alps, sentiments such as are attributed to Empedocles on the day before his ascent of Mt. Etna. "My dearest Clough," Arnold writes, "these are damned times—everything is against one—the height to which knowledge is come, the spread of luxury, our physical enervation, the absence of great *natures*, the unavoidable contact with millions of small ones, newspapers, cities, light profligate friends, moral desperadoes like Carlyle, our own selves, and the sickening consciousness of our difficulties. . . ." So Empedocles fumes against the "swelling evil of this time,"

since all
Clouds and grows daily worse in Sicily,
Since broils tear us in twain, since this new swarm
Of sophists has got empire in our schools . . . .

The only difference is that Arnold adds: "but for God's sake let us neither be fanatics nor yet chalf [sic] blown by the wind but let us be ὡς ὁ φρόνιμος διαρίσειεν [as the prudent man would define] and not as any one else διαρίσειεν [would define]."[12] Thus, when Arnold reached the top of the mountain, he did not, like Empedocles, throw himself into a volcano. Rather, in rejecting Obermann, he threw his own personal Empedocles into a volcano and came back down, a whole man, to lead a useful life in the cities of the plain. Thus, although in one sense *Empedocles on Etna* dramatizes what Arnold did, in another it dramatizes what he did not do. It dramatizes what he was saved from doing by the fact that he did it vicariously in the realm of art.

Though I have said that this crisis in the Bernese Alps was the most important spiritual crisis of Arnold's entire life, one ought to observe that the rejection of one's Ordinary Self in favor of his True or Best Self is not something that is accomplished once and for all. Rather it has to be enacted over and over again, and thus at various times in Arnold's life we get repetitions of this crisis. An important one occurred in October 1853, when he rejected *Empedocles on Etna* from the third volume of his poems and wrote the Preface of 1853 explaining why. This is a kind of acknowledgment that since 1849 he had lapsed back into some sympathy with his hero and felt the necessity of a second public exorcism of his spirit. There was also a significant anticipation of the crisis in November 1848, about which I will say something in a moment; and there were further repetitions of it almost every time Arnold wrote an elegy. This is, indeed, why Arnold is so characteristically an elegiac poet, because the elegy is the form in which, under the guise of the death and rebirth of his subject, he can accomplish the death of his Ordinary Self and the rebirth of his Best Self. Almost all poets use the elegy as a means of talking about themselves, but Arnold differs from poets like Milton and Shelley in that he comes to bury Caesar not to praise him. Whereas they use the elegy as an instrument of self-pity and self-vindication, asserting that what is lost here on earth will be restored in another sphere, Arnold uses it as a means of self-criticism and self-transformation, asserting that what is imperfect here on earth can be replaced, here on earth, by something better. We have seen him do this in the elegy on Obermann, and he also does it in the elegies on Charlotte Brontë, his brother William Delafield Arnold, Clough, and the poet Heine. Let us examine briefly the elegy on Clough and that on Heine.

Arnold first read Heine in 1848, about the time of the Marguerite affair, and initially he was "disgusted." "The Byronism of a German," he wrote to his mother, "of a man trying to be gloomy, cynical, impassioned, *moqueur*, etc., all *à la fois* . . . is the most ridiculous thing in the world. . . . I see the French call this Heine a 'Voltaire au claire de lune,' which is very happy." It so happened, however, that the English were experiencing a fit of sanctimonious horror about Heine, Carlyle calling him a "filthy, foetid sausage of spoiled victuals," and Kingsley replying to his daughter's question, "Who is Heine?" with the words, "A very wicked man, my dear." Obviously, rather than agree with such persons, Arnold would be the champion of Heine, and in 1861 he assured Clough that he was a "far more profitable" study than Tennyson.[13] He was impressed by the picture of the poet lying for the last eight years of his life on a sick-bed in Paris and sending forth from his "mattress-grave" arrowy shafts of irony and satire. In this sense he was a very symbol of the modern spirit—the spirit which, undaunted by evil but unable to reply any longer with the true Byronic thunder, replied with mockery and laughter.

The trouble is that by 1862-63, when the poem was written, Arnold no longer admired mockery and laughter as he once had, and so, after a very brief tribute, he asks the question,

What, then, so harsh and malign,
Heine! distils from thy life?
Poisons the peace of thy grave?

The answer is that Heine had every other gift but Love and, wanting that, also wanted Charm. Charm, we are now told, is what "makes

[the] song of the poet divine." Well, it may be so. We can, of course, remember a time in Arnold's youth when it was Joy which made the song of the poet divine, and we may suspect that Charm is simply the watered-down, mid-Victorian equivalent of Joy. We may also think that Arnold has offended more people by his Charm, which is now known as "smiling insolence," than by any other quality he possesses. Nevertheless, it is true that just at this time he was very much interested in acquiring Charm. He was eager to *get at* the English public. "Such a public as it is," he wrote to his mother, "and such a work as one wants to do with it! Partly nature, partly time and study have also by this time taught me thoroughly the precious truth that everything turns upon one's exercising the power of *persuasion, of charm*; that without this all fury, energy, reasoning power, acquirement, are thrown away and only render their owner more miserable. Even in one's ridicule one must preserve a sweetness and good-humour."[14] Heine did not preserve a sweetness and good-humour and therefore Heine must be rejected, and this is exactly what Arnold did, in words of one syllable, at the end of the poem. "Bitter and strange," he says, "was the life / Of Heine . . . may a life / Other and milder be mine!"

Indeed, Arnold felt that he could put his finger on the precise moment when he and Heine had parted company, and it was the same moment when he had parted from Obermann. For Heine is presented in the poem in the same terms as Obermann—those of the dilemma solitude vs. the world—and the crucial moment of his life was a time in his youth when he had ascended the Hartz mountains. Arnold describes this moment and then comments:

Goethe too had been there.
In the long-past winter he came
To the frozen Hartz, with his soul
Passionate, eager—his youth
All in ferment!—but he
Destined to work and to live
Left it, and thou, alas!
Only to laugh and to die.

The moment which Heine had described in the *Reisebilder* and

Goethe in his poem *Harzreise im Winter*, Arnold had described in the *Stanzas in Memory of the Author of 'Obermann.'* In that moment he had chosen Goethe rather than Heine as his guide, and his elegy on Heine is a kind of prayer of thanksgiving that he had not done otherwise. For Heine's reward was to be buried in a curiously ambiguous grave in Montmartre cemetery, whereas Arnold was alive and on the threshold of a new career.

About the same time that Arnold wrote the elegy on Heine, Clough died, and it is a striking thing that Arnold could not write his elegy without ascending an eminence. This time it was the Cumnor hills. Writing to Mrs. Clough to thank her for sending him some of her husband's poems, he said, "I shall take them with me to Oxford, where I shall go after Easter:—and there, among the Cumner hills where we have so often rambled, I shall be able to think him over as I would wish."[15] The thing Arnold needed to think over was why it was that Clough's life had been a failure. In their Rugby and Oxford days everybody would have predicted that he, rather than the supercilious Arnold, would have had the brilliant career. But in point of fact he had not. After a few original but rather mischievous poems, he had thrown up his tutorship and then his fellowship at Oriel, partly out of irritation with the Thirty-Nine Articles but more especially out of a desire to help in the work of social betterment. In May 1848 he had gone over to Paris to watch the Revolution, and in the following spring he was in Rome observing Garibaldi fight the French. All this was very glamorous. It was far less glamorous to do as Arnold had done—stay at home, marry the daughter of an English judge, and become an Inspector of Her Majesty's Schools. Yet now, in 1861, Clough was dead with little accomplished, whereas Arnold was increasingly acknowledged as an authentic poet of the day, was elected Professor of Poetry at the University of Oxford, and at that moment was delivering the lectures on translating Homer which would lay the basis of a distinguished critical reputation.

Thus, as Arnold thought his friend over at Easter, he felt again that he could put his finger on the exact moment when he and Clough had parted company. This time it was November 1848, when he had returned to Oxford from Switzerland and found Clough who had just renounced his fellowship and published his *Bothie of Tober-na-Vuolich*, the hero of the hour. "I have been at Oxford the last two days," Arnold wrote to his friend, "and hearing Sellar and the rest of that clique who know neither life nor themselves rave about your poem gave me a strong almost bitter feeling with respect to them, the age, even you. Yes I said to myself something tells me I can, if need be, at last dispense with them all, even with him: better that, than be sucked for an hour even into the Time Stream in which they and he plunge and bellow."[16] And it was at this point that he "took up Obermann and refuged myself with him in his forest against your Zeit Geist." Given Arnold's penchant for symbolic action, it seems to me very likely that he actually did take Obermann up into the Cumnor hills and meditate on his reasons for separating from Clough. For we know that there was actually a slight estrangement between the two friends beginning at this time. Clough complained about it in 1853, and Arnold, writing a long "historical" letter in reply, admitted that "there was one time indeed—shortly after you had published the Bothie—that I felt a strong disposition to intellectual seclusion, and to the barring out all influences that I felt troubled without advancing me." He went on to explain that where he thought Clough going wrong was that he never would "resolve to be thyself," but was always wondering whether he shouldn't be this or that other person *qui ne vous valaient pas*. "You have I am convinced lost infinite time in this way: it is what I call your morbid conscientiousness—you are the most conscientious man I ever knew: but on some lines morbidly so, and it spoils your action."[17]

This estrangement of the two friends is dramatically represented in *The Scholar-Gipsy*, where the scene is the Cumnor hills and the imaginative date is 1848. In the opening stanza of the poem the poet is lying in the high half-reaped field and is dismissing his friend to the world of action for which he yearns.

> Go, for they call you, shepherd from the hill;
>   Go, shepherd, and untie the wattled cotes!
>   No longer leave thy wistful flock unfed,
>   Nor let thy bawling fellows rack their throats.

He only adjures him, once "the fields are still, / And the tired men and dogs all gone to rest,"—that is, once the revolutionary movements of 1848 are over—to return and again begin the quest. And he declares that he will wait for him till sundown. Sundown proved to be just one year, for it was one year later, in September 1849, that Arnold rejected Obermann and declared, "I in the world must live." This decision is reflected in the poem in the poet's shift of locus, for although in the beginning of the poem he is in the high half-reaped field and is soon united with the Scholar-Gipsy in a poetic vision, by the end of the poem he is crying, "Fly *our* paths, *our* feverish contact fly!" as though he were located in the world. The shift comes at the mid-point of the poem when he cries, "But what—I dream!" and by acknowledging that the Scholar-Gipsy does not haunt these fields but is buried in some country churchyard, falls from the level of poetic vision into the phenomenal world.

At this point the problem becomes very complex and very interesting. For in the poem Arnold says that the book which lies beside him in the grass is Glanvill's book—*The Vanity of Dogmatizing*, which contains the legend of the Scholar-Gipsy which Arnold proceeds to recount in the poem. But in his letter of November 1848 he says, "I . . . took up Obermann, and refuged myself with him in his forest against your Zeit Geist," and whether or not Arnold did in fact take Obermann up into the Cumnor hills and have him beside him in the grass, we know that from 1847-49 Obermann was "the master of [Arnold's] wandering youth." The days when he read Glanvill and perhaps took him up into the Cumnor hills were 1845-47, and the shift from one to the other is one of the most important in Arnold's spiritual development. For Obermann is as different in spirit from Glanvill and the Scholar-Gipsy as the Bernese Alps are from the Cumnor hills, and it is a momentous fact that Arnold, with the help of Marguerite, had gravitated from one to the other. In 1849 he had no reasonable alternative except to come down from the Alps and reside in the world, but in November 1848 it must have seemed as if he could have remained forever with the Scholar-Gipsy among the Cumnor hills.

We see, then, how important this crisis was to Arnold, and so it is no wonder that when he came to write Clough's elegy he took as his subject not Clough's death in 1861 but his going away from Oxford in 1848. For in Arnold's view the moment when Clough "died" was the moment when he threw himself into the Time Stream and made himself subject to change and death. And that was the moment when, abandoning the quest for the ideal, he had given himself up to direct social action in the world. Of course, Arnold in 1849 had done something similar, but in all these poems Arnold makes two distinctions between himself and Clough. The first is that he was driven by fate, whereas "Thyrsis of his own will went away." And the second is that he intended so to live in the world as to remain unspotted by it. But the question now is how far either he or Clough has succeeded in doing this. Has he been so long in the world that he cannot recover the poetic power signalized by the elm? For of course, the problem is, not whether the elm is still standing but whether Arnold can see it. Ultimately, he does, and curiously enough, the way he sees it is by writing *Thyrsis*. We all remember the beautiful stanza beginning, "O easy access to the hearer's grace," which speaks of how easy it was for the ancient elegist to "flute his friend, like Orpheus, from the grave." Far different it is for the modern poet, and yet, though Arnold augurs ill of the attempt, he has no recourse but to try.

> Yet, Thyrsis, let me give my grief its hour
>   In the old haunt, and find our tree-topp'd hill!
> Who, if not I, for questing here hath power?

What these lines indicate is that Arnold's quest for the tree will be accomplished by giving his grief its hour, that is, by writing an elegy. And so, a hundred lines after the beginning of the poem we get an elegy within an elegy which has as its purpose to determine whether the elegist can sing. That he can we learn from the sudden cry, "The tree! the tree!" which he sees on its lonely ridge against the sky. The sight of the tree is the elegiac reversal in the poem—the moment when the poet turns from the negative to the positive aspect of his theme—but it is very striking that here it takes the form not of the death and rebirth of Clough but of the loss and recovery of the tree. The tree is still standing, and Clough did wrong to forsake it.

For when Arnold turns to include Clough in his discovery, "Hear it, O Thyrsis, still our tree is there!" we are told that Thyrsis cannot hear it, and his death in Italy is taken as a second symbolic desertion of the Cumnor fields. The harshness of this conclusion is somewhat mitigated in the final stanzas, but the poem is still so critical of Clough that Arnold wisely did not send to Mrs. Clough the product of his reflections in the Cumnor hills.

The end of this story is that after his sojourn in the world Arnold reascended the hills from which formerly he had come down. We have seen him doing so in *Thyrsis*, and there are further examples in *Rugby Chapel* and *Obermann Once More*. Of course, they are not exactly the same hills as before. That in *Thyrsis* differs from its counterpart in *The Scholar-Gipsy* not only by the signal-elm, which does not occur in the earlier poem, but also by that abstract institution, the Throne of Truth. The mountain in *Rugby Chapel*, unlike that in *Empedocles on Etna* and *Resignation*, is no longer a place where poets brood in isolation, but rather where the Servants of God help others up the mountain so that they too may be saved. And finally, in *Obermann Once More* we encounter a new Obermann so different from the old that we hardly recognize either his appearance or what he has to say. He tells his disciple that the age of skepticism is past and a new age of faith about to dawn, and he urges Arnold, though more than half his years be past, to give himself to communicating this faith to the world. Thus, if Arnold was once on Mt. Etna or the Alps, he is now on Mt. Sinai or Mt. Pisgah, and is preparing to lead the Children of Israel to the Promised Land by means of *Literature and Dogma*.

Finally, let me remind you that in one of Arnold's earliest poems he had imaged his situation by a mountain, saying that in this way he was *in utrumque paratus*, "prepared for either alternative," either that he should have to ascend by lonely pureness to God or descend to his brother-world toiling below. Ultimately, both alternatives were true, and it was by ascending and descending, by participation and withdrawal, that Arnold mediated between solitude and the world.

[1] *The Letters of Matthew Arnold to Arthur Hugh Clough*, ed. H. F. Lowry (Oxford, 1932), p. 110. Hereafter cited as *Letters to Clough*.

[2] *Ibid.*, p. 95.

[3] *Obermann Once More*, l. 39. Arnold's poetry is quoted from *The Poetical Works of Matthew Arnold*, ed. C. B. Tinker and H. F. Lowry (Oxford, 1950).

[4] C. B. Tinker and H. F. Lowry, *The Poetry of Matthew Arnold: A Commentary* (Oxford, 1950), p. 287. Hereafter cited as Tinker and Lowry.

[5] *Too Late*, l.4.

[6] *Letters to Clough*, pp. 110-11.

[7] *Poetical Works*, p. 499.

[8] *Letters to Clough*, p. 92.

[9] [Étienne Pivert] de Sénancour, *Obermann*, nouvelle édition revue et corrigée, avec un préface par George Sand (Paris, 1852), pp. 6-7.

[10] Tinker and Lowry, p. 271.

[11] *Letters to Clough*, pp. 109-10.

[12] *Ibid.*, p. 111.

[13] *Letters of Matthew Arnold, 1848-1888*, ed. G. W. E. Russell (New York, 1895), I, 11; Sol Liptzin, *The English Legend of Heinrich Heine* (New York, 1954), and "The English Reception of Heine," *Victorian Newsletter*, No. 11 (1957), 14-16; Walter Houghton, *The Victorian Frame of Mind* (New Haven, 1957), pp. 172-73; *Letters to Clough*, p. 154.

[14] *Letters*, I, 234.

[15] *Letters to Clough*, p. 160.

[16] *Ibid.*, p. 95.

[17] *Ibid.*, pp. 129-30.

WARREN D. ANDERSON

Types of the Classical in Arnold, Tennyson, and Browning

I N T H A T N O T A B L E A G E of poetry which gained its first
mature powers at the nineteenth century's mid-point, Arnold,
Tennyson, and Browning ruled their several provinces of the
sensibilities like medieval barons. At feast or council they would
meet civilly enough, visors raised, but for the most part each kept to
his own territories.

All three, however, felt compelled to meet the past on terms quite
unlike those of Miniver Cheevy. The legacy they could not but ac-
knowledge, as grateful heirs or unthankful rebels, was that of a
classical tradition. Standards and formulas, attitudes and styles deriv-
ing from the poetry of Greece or Rome still confronted poets with a
memorial outlasting bronze, not subject to time's corrosion nor
quickly toppled by even the most powerful of vagrant impulses
from a vernal wood. None of our three writers was so tame-spirited
as to content himself with being a mere continuator: the mantles of
Gray and Cowper might be honest cloth, but they were thinly lined.
Neither did any of the three turn wholly away from the classical
experience. Even Robert Browning attacked Aeschylus partly by
embracing Euripides.

Studies of borrowings from Greek and Latin sources have not
been wanting. The difficulty is that identifying verse and chapter
does not help us very much to understand the larger design. Now
the wind sets from another quarter; yet even such admirable studies
as those of DeVane on Browning's anti-Hellenism or Professor
Stange on Tennyson's mythologizing take a larger view at the expense of any extended comparisons among the three poets—nor has

Matthew Arnold fared any better in this respect. The present paper suggests certain possible guide-lines for such a comparative study, working toward a Victorian typology of attitudes.

The quest for definitions brings little comfort. Arnold was noticeably wary of defining the classical, and the newly imported term *Klassizismus* wrung his withers. Tennyson apparently never felt that semantic exercise could strengthen him; and so far as Browning ever showed such a conviction, it makes itself known in contrasts with Christianity where one quickly sees which is cast as Hyperion and which as the satyr. As for Victorian poetic theory, at mid-century criticism had not yet found its voice. If any echo still reached men's minds from an earlier generation it was Goethe's dictum that the classical equates with health, the Romantic with sickness. Since neither poetry nor poetics will oblige us, we may accept provisionally a definition of the classical as passion and order in a relationship of tension that, as Heraclitus knew, makes the structure one.

We look first to the formative years for a clue. After a period of study at home the young Matthew Arnold went to various tutors, whom he annoyed as only the lazy clever student can, and came before long under his father's new and enlightened regime at Rugby School. In what concerns the classical, Oxford's effect upon him was negligible. Fox How (the Arnolds' summer home) and Rugby are the dynamic centers. The same figure dominates either setting, endlessly energetic. A contemporary's joking reference to "David, the son of Goliath" has its truth; yet Matthew Arnold learned from his father two things that no one else could have taught him so well. The first was the sense of classical antiquity as a heart-shaking presence; the second, an awareness of moral analogies that fused past and present into a single paradigm.

The children of George Clayton Tennyson likewise carried the mark of a father's extraordinary nature; we need not be concerned with its more harrowing aspects. Unlike young Matthew, Alfred was his father's favorite. For him Dr. Tennyson, a master of Greek and Latin, poured out his learning. The boy went away for a short time to a grammar school; there he passed through an ordeal like the nightmare experience of John Anthony Froude.[1] Tennyson's only pleasant memory of his ordeal, says Grierson, "was the music of the Latin words *sonus desilientis aquae*." Though the phrase has been misquoted, its source is clear: it comes from the *Fasti* of Ovid, a versified kalendar of religious ritual and myth.[2]

The instinctive choice of author and passage shadows things to come. Among all classical poets Ovid is preeminently the master of sound and color. His smoothly slipping verse, inimitably deft, possesses an ultimate polish. To be sure, no other writer of antiquity caught emotional nuances with equal insight, and his shorter poems are by no means shapeless. He lacks, however, a true architectonic sense and a concern for moral meaning. His longer works reveal themselves as overwhelmingly episodic. The only value that he recognizes is love, and his verse trembles with a passion far more often illicit than innocent. Whatever the immediate theme, he devised for its expression language of incomparable sensuous richness and grace, language so artful that it seemed unpremeditated, inevitable—the very voice of poetry as craftsmanship. These qualities made Ovid's *Metamorphoses* the fountainhead of Renaissance art; in a considerable degree they are the same traits which were to mark Tennyson's verse with distinction.

The context of the words that so charmed the unhappy schoolboy has its own significance. Ovid's passage tells how Dis, lord of the lower realms, carried off the lovely Persephone as she gathered flowers in the vale of Enna, leaving Ceres (the Greek Demeter) to search despairingly for her vanished child. This same story prompted the first and almost the last of Tennyson's frequent excursions into mythology. For his earliest translation into English he took a passage from the *De Raptu Proserpinae* of Claudian, and near the end of his life he came back to the theme: "Demeter and Persephone," to which we shall recur, is his last major treatment of myth.

"There is a place in a shaded valley," says Ovid, "well moistened by the spattering water that leaps down from high above":

Valle sub umbrosa locus est, aspergine multa
uvidus ex alto desilientis aquae.

If any English poet can match this music Tennyson can, and he alone. But the Ovidian fragment suggests another factor and another poet. Ovid actually meant little to Tennyson's mature command of his art; even Vergil contributed only the affinities of delicacy and tender melancholy that repeatedly reinforce the poetic tone, though this was no minor contribution. In terms of specific influence the sovereign figure is Theocritus, greatest among the Hellenistic poets. As a favored vehicle Theocritus chose neither full-scale literary epic nor the opposite extreme of epigram, the two verse media especially cultivated by Alexandrian scholarship. Instead he devised the *eidullion*, the "miniature poem" that we call an idyll. Anong its sub-types was the *epullion*, or "epic in miniature," and it is this which accounts for Tennyson's choice of the title *Idylls of the King* for a major work.[3] Plotting a middle course between the unity that literary epic must possess and the shapelessness of mere verse narrative, he compromised: his choice was the episode raised to a new level of effectiveness through command of a Theocritean richness, elegance, and precision. Into this chosen setting he fitted the multitude of chiseled lines and phrases that a truly Ovidian skill had placed at his disposing; and if the result is artifice, it is seldom mere artificiality.

Much of Tennyson's classicism derives from these origins. Although he was uniquely sensitive to the music that first had caught his ear in the verses of Horace and Ovid, he shows little concern with any dimension other than the aesthetic in classical poetry. For him Greek and Latin had originally been disciplines, suggesting no larger pattern of meaning. He does, indeed, echo in individual passages what he believed to be the characteristic Homeric or Vergilian note. The resource he cannot command is a broader view of the past: despite all the felicities of tone and cadence, the classical beauties of his style remain largely isolated. Tennyson is the poet of those who look upon the masterworks of Greek and Latin literature as a treasury of telling phrases or passages to be excerpted.[4]

Robert Browning remembered being sung to sleep in his father's arms with the gentle Greek lyrics of Anacreon. Despite this happy beginning he came to the actual study of Greek unaccountably late, during two years at the University of London. Latin, on the other hand, he had begun at the usual very early stage. His formal educa-

tion was notably incomplete and irregular: much of his knowledge
of ancient literature can only have been self-taught. His conception
of the classical lacked centrality, and by the same token the classical
past had no real importance for him.

The development of a Robert Browning trained (let us say) at
Rugby and Balliol defies even remote conjecture. It does seem clear
that the classical training of the universities had little effect on any of
these three poets; and for Browning the decisive factor was his marriage.[5] Elizabeth Barrett had come to regard the great things of
Greek literature more and more as attempts to grasp the truth later
revealed by Christianity. Her enthusiasm combined with his own reaction against Arnold's praise of Aeschylus and Sophocles in the
1853 Preface, and the combination proved to have results not less
varied than strange. Most immediately it brought about Browning's
advocacy of Euripides, with whom he shared certain virtues and
faults. By 1855 it had moved him to suggest the higher merits of
Christianity in "Cleon" (an undistinguished reply to Arnold's "Empedocles on Etna") and in various other poems of the *Men and
Women* collection. Eventually, a decade and more after his wife's
death, it would prompt a double retelling of the Alcestis story in *Ba-
laustion's Adventure* and a translation of the *Agamemnon*. The first
of these takes some warmth from the remembered presence of Elizabeth, that Alcestis whom an impetuous champion had once rescued
from her death-like imprisonment. The second has nothing to com-
mend it, least of all its motive, for the preface reveals a clear desire to
prove that Arnold had been wrong about the glories of Aeschylus.
"The Browning version" is assault with what was meant to be a
deadly weapon: fortunately it exemplifies a concept of translation so
completely wrong-headed that it has been placed on the shelf as a
curiosity and rendered harmless.[6]

We may well doubt whether Browning could ever have attained
the balance and perspective that must form a part at least of the classical. His "Artemis Prologizes," written before he had met his wife, is
more fantastic than anything similar that followed it. Sir Henry
Jones's comment on Elizabeth applies almost equally well to her husband: "No poet ever had less of the Greek spirit of measure and pro-

portion." The same critic has well said that "for Browning, there was no form which the human soul could take that was too strange, complex, monstrous, magnificent, commonplace and drab, in its hate or love or in any other passion, to be interesting in the artistic and purely impersonal sense."[7] Of course, this may be nothing less than the premise of greatness: such was Leonardo, following grotesquely misshapen men through the streets to fix their every feature on his mind. If so, it seems to constitute in both instances a peculiarly Renaissance type of greatness. The main cast of Browning's temperament, whether we call it Renaissance or Gothic, was profoundly unclassical. Learning he possessed in helter-skelter abundance, and incredible energy of mind as well. What he had quite deliberately rejected as "antique" and inadequate was the spirit of the past; and in this dispensation too the letter kills, but the spirit gives life.

Matthew Arnold's relationships with the classical experience seem to show at least three stages, all achieved before mid-century or very shortly thereafter. One notes the usual initial phase of experimentation, then a time of near-involvement with the elemental powers of the classical, and finally a withdrawal to the safety of an objective vantage-point.[8] It is against this complex background that his classicism must be viewed. We shall not rehearse here the arguments for the existence of such a background: for present purposes there is likely to be more value in an account of certain respects in which Tennyson's mature work suggests a comparison or contrast on classical grounds with that of Arnold.

Lucretius, the Epicurean poet of atomic theory, impressed both men deeply. Arnold never made any real headway with the major work, so long contemplated, that was to center about him. Portions of it, however, were salvaged for "Empedocles"; and the important essay of 1858, "On the Modern Element in Literature," contains an extensive analysis of Lucretius. This critique clearly shows Arnold's rejection of the absurd claim that love-potions drove the poet into periodic madness. For Arnold he typified the overly active mind; to present him as actually unbalanced would have crippled the argument.

Some years later there appeared a radically different treatment of the same theme. Tennyson's "Lucretius" depends directly on the gossip of aphrodisiacs and insanity. Not realizing what he is drinking, the poet suffers fearful erotic dreams that impel him to take his life. One wonders why Tennyson felt it necessary to follow a tradition which Arnold so pointedly avoided. Professor Buckley has written that "Lucretius is placed in a society no longer open to wonder, but bent rather upon the total destruction of the imagination and intellect," an age which therefore eludes the intellectual's powers of vision.[9] Tennyson's despairing comments elsewhere offer ample support for this view, not found in the poem itself; they show us that he has taken the past as a paradigm of the later Victorian age. We may suggest an added point. By making the effect of aphrodisiacs a main structural element, Tennyson gained an outlet for that overheated and underachieved Eros which intermittently marks his poetry.[10]

Arnold here provides the most emphatic contrast imaginable. To cite only two instances, he showed himself utterly incapable of understanding what Wagner had done in creating *Tristan und Isolde*—after an evening at the opera in Berlin his only comment was "I handled the story better"—and he lacked any sympathy with Swinburne. The absence of carnality from his own poetic thought is striking. As for dealings with Lucretius, Tennyson emerges more creditably in that he uses the Roman poet to voice his protest against the contemporary scene. Arnold, less single-minded, seemed unable to decide between two contradictory views: either Lucretius represented his age as a typical victim of "the predominance of thought . . . in modern epochs," or he could not be its true interpreter because he was morbid. Readers are left comfortless here; yet it does at any rate appear that quite different motives prompted Arnold and Tennyson to use Lucretius as a *persona*.

Mythology provides another ground of difference. Tennyson not only presents classical myth more extensively and elaborately than Arnold; he also goes beyond the limits of his original—beyond the very bounds of antiquity, in fact—as Arnold never does. Here he is close to Robert Browning and perhaps closer still to Elizabeth, who (for example) saw Prometheus not as Shelley's humanistic Titan but as a prefiguring of the Christian Saviour. So in "Demeter and Persephone" the aged Tennyson has his earth-goddess foresee the rule of "younger kindlier Gods," hinting at the reign of Christian love. His whole handling of this poem goes beyond the classical story that first had caught his imagination in Ovid's verses, more than seventy years earlier.

With Arnold the case is quite otherwise. He too had come near the end of his life when he sought out the Demeter myth. The occasion did not lack Christian significance, moreover: Arnold created this last of his major poems, "Westminster Abbey," as a memorial to the Abbey's famous Dean, his old friend Arthur Stanley. Never before had Arnold used myth so extensively; never before had he been so willing to let it speak for itself. Having chosen the Homeric Hymn to Demeter, he felt no need to Christianize it or to write imaginary sequels. By contrast, Tennyson was voicing the convictions of a lifetime in his comment on "Demeter and Persephone": "When I write an antique like this," he told his son, "I must put it into a frame —something modern about it. It is no use giving a mere *réchauffé* of old legends."[11] Nothing could be less Arnoldian than this attitude.

The all-embracing, enigmatic archetypal figure that is Ulysses brings together the three poets of our typology for a final comparison. Once again Tennyson furnishes the *locus classicus*; and here we shall be dealing with what must be one of the most controversial of all major Victorian poems. It is doubtful whether any two scholars have ever reached detailed agreement on the exegesis of "Ulysses." A particularly vexing question concerns the ethical position which it sets forth. One wonders how to interpret the sneering impatience with wife and son and other assorted *impedimenta* of domesticity, the claim (not present in the first draft) to have "enjoyed all times greatly," the proposal to follow the star of knowledge over the horizon's edge, the whole restless longing to be outward bound.

On this matter some attention should be paid to the heresies of E. J. Chiasson, who has eloquently stated his minority opinion.[12] Tennyson, he tells us, is not using this poem as a sounding-board for his own homilies on suitable reactions to the death of a close friend. Quite the contrary: the poet deplores such unconjugal, antisocial vagabondage and finds it irresponsible in the highest degree. This thesis takes itself a little too seriously—for one thing, the poem has a genuine and compelling excitement—but we ought not therefore to reject it out of hand. The statement "I am a part of all that I have met" comes very oddly indeed, if we insist on taking it as a Tennysonian credo. Actually it seems far better suited to the works of Robert Browning, whose infinitely faceted personality lights his whole poetic universe. This one indication, slight as it is, should constitute sufficient warning that any simplified reading of "Ulysses" will oversimplify the poem's complexities. Tennyson's lines may relate to those conflicting impulses which he himself had been quick to recognize; he had set them forth clearly in his earliest poem of bereavement, "The Two Voices." Of these impulses, the death-wish finally recurs in "Tithonus"; "Ulysses," from the same general period, echoes the victorious life-urge of "The Two Voices," but it displays a far different spirit.

The difference may find an explanation in Tennyson's convictions. He was certain that eventually, if one persevered, the discords of reality would somehow give way to ideal harmony. Thus his Ulysses must sail ever onward; nor is the voyage pointless, as many have argued. Ulysses looks forward to the chance of touching at the "Happy Isles" and of seeing "the great Achilles, whom we knew." But Homer's Achilles is far from the Islands of the Blest. Death has taken him, as death took Arthur Hallam, and he moves among the dim ghosts in Hades' realm. Tennyson refuses to hear this voice of death. His thoughts now seem to go back not to Homer but to Vergil's cyclic vision (*Ecl.* 4.36) of a new *magnus Achilles*. Arnold too recalled this passage from the *Eclogues*, as "Palladium" shows; yet he never assigned Ulysses a poetic role of any importance. To him this Dantesque Romantic figure symbolized knowledge as experience, a knowledge markedly inferior to that possessed by the poet. His clearcut position offers a final contrast with the ambivalent attitude manifested by Tennyson, who is perhaps not so clearly "past the hesitancy of 'The Two Voices' " as Chiasson claims at the conclusion of his argument.

We have suggested three approaches to the classical: Browning's mixed feelings and his fundamental eccentricity, reinforced by the haphazardness of his education, that set him forever patching and cobbling at the antique without a saner perspective; Tennyson's mastery of individual effects and his refashioning of myth as personal expression; and, as a basis for comparison, Arnold's successive dealings with the past that move toward involvement and then avoid it, never rivalling Browning's energy or Tennyson's rich workmanship but commanding an overview that neither could achieve. All three poets, as they exemplify the shifting balance of passion and order, are in their fashion faithful or faithless to the classical experience; and for all three this experience provides us with an index of being, an Ariadne's thread tracing the labyrinth of Victorian poetry.

[1] A vivid account is given by Waldo H. Dunn, *James Anthony Froude: A Biography*, I (Oxford, 1961), 31-38.

[2] H. J. C. Grierson in *The Cambridge History of English Literature*, ed. Sir A. W. Ward and A. R. Waller (Cambridge, 1953), XIII, ii, 22. *Fasti* 4.427-28 ends with *desilientis aquae*; the text is reproduced below.

[3] See J. A. K. Thomson, *The Classical Background of English Literature* (London, 1948), pp. 78, 237; also, and more particularly, the same author's *Classical Influences on English Poetry* (London, 1951), pp. 193-95. In *Mythology and the Romantic Tradition* (Cambridge, Mass., 1937) Douglas Bush has several valuable references to Tennyson's knowledge and use of Theocritus: see p. 204 and n. 12, also p. 244 and n. 54.

[4] J. F. A. Pyre (*The Formation of Tennyson's Style* [Madison, 1921], p. 100) speaks for his time in saying that Tennyson was "firmly under the discipline of that *aurea mediocritas* which constitutes the classic message in art." Sir Oliver Elton's remarks (*A Survey of English Literature 1830-1880* [London, 1920], I, 335-36, 338-39), though far superior, come from the same period and bear its mark. Even Grierson (above, n. 2), p. 45, contends that Tennyson achieved "the reproduction of the very soul of some Greek and Roman poets. . . ." For a balanced judgment we must go to Professor Bush, pp. 197-228. The sections of his work which deal with Arnold and Browning (pp. 245-64, 358-85) are equally indispensable; the special bibliographies should also be noted.

[5] See W. C. DeVane's careful study, "Browning and the Spirit of Greece," in *Nineteenth-Century Studies*, ed. Herbert Davis, W. C. DeVane, and R. C. Bald (Ithaca, 1940), pp. 179-98.

[6] Robert Spindler, *Robert Browning und die Antike* (Leipzig, 1930), ac-

tually calls the translations masterpieces worthy to stand beside the originals. Some value may attach to his further claim that Browning as a young man saw the classics through the eyes of Shelley. Spindler's book is reviewed in *The Year's Work in English Studies* (1931), pp. 281-82.

[7] Sir Henry Jones in *The Cambridge History* (above, n. 2), pp. 71, 64. He also argues strongly (pp. 66-67) that Browning's characters lack objectivity. Professor Buckley has suggested to me that some would feel Browning was trying to become more objective in his mature work; and certainly one recognizes a difference between *Pauline* and the later poems. Elton (above, n. 4), p. 388, unaccountably describes "Artemis Prologizes" as a "lovely and stately Hellenic." I may somehow have failed to see the classical merits of this poem, praised by Professor Bush as well (pp. 361-62).

[8] I have sought to show these stages in *Matthew Arnold and the Classical Tradition* (Ann Arbor, 1965).

[9] Jerome H. Buckley, *Tennyson: The Growth of a Poet* (Cambridge, Mass., 1960), p. 196.

[10] In "Lucretius," Tennyson's conscious attitude toward the erotic was of course condemnatory, as Walter E. Houghton has pointed out (*The Victorian Frame of Mind* [New Haven, 1957], p. 371, n. 85 to ch. 13). See the valuable discussion of this poem by Professor Bush (pp. 213-16), who contends that it is "not a mosaic of beautiful lines but a whole. . . ." As such it forms an exception to his regular procedure of substituting a "continual succession of splendid moments" (Lascelles Abercrombie, quoted in Bush, p. 213) for unified poems.

[11] Quoted in Buckley, p. 246; reference in Bush, p. 206, n. 16.

[12] E. J. Chiasson, "Tennyson's 'Ulysses'—A Re-interpretation," in *Critical Essays on the Poetry of Tennyson*, ed. John Killham (New York, 1960), pp. 164-73, esp. 172-73.

LIONEL STEVENSON

The Relativity of Truth
in Victorian Fiction

I N AN IMPORTANT PASSAGE IN *Modern Painters*
(1843), Ruskin wrote as follows:

> The difference between ideas of truth and of imitation lies
> chiefly in the following points: First,—Imitation can only be
> of something material, but truth has reference to statements
> both of the qualities of material things, and of emotions, im-
> pressions, and thoughts. There is a moral as well as material
> truth,—a truth of impression as well as of form,—of thought
> as well as of matter; and the truth of impression and thought is
> a thousand times the more important of the two. Hence, truth
> is a term of universal application, but imitation is limited to
> that narrow field of art which takes cognizance only of material
> things. Secondly,—Truth may be stated by any signs or sym-
> bols which have a definite signification in the minds of those to
> whom they are addressed, although such signs be themselves
> no image nor likeness of anything. Whatever can excite in the
> mind the conception of certain facts, can give ideas of truth,
> though it be in no degree the imitation or resemblance of those
> facts.... Ideas of imitation, of course, require the likeness of
> the object. They speak to the perceptive faculties only: truth to
> the conceptive. (Vol. I, Pt. 2, 1, Ch. 5)

Ruskin was here writing primarily about painting, but he stated a
theory that was becoming of urgent importance in literature also.
Twenty years later, Arnold expressed a kindred notion with more
vivacity, in the preface to his *Essays in Criticism*:

> To try and approach truth on one side after another, not to
> strive or cry, nor to persist in pressing forward, on any one side,

with violence and self-will,—it is only thus, it seems to me, that mortals may hope to gain any vision of the mysterious Goddess, whom we shall never see except in outline, but only thus even in outline. He who will do nothing but fight impetuously towards her on his own, one, favourite, particular line, is inevitably destined to run his head into the folds of the black robe in which she is wrapped.

Just at the same time as Arnold, Walter Pater wrote in his essay on Coleridge:

> To the modern spirit nothing is, or can be rightly known, except relatively and under conditions. The philosophical conception of the relative has been developed in modern times through the influence of the sciences of observation. Those sciences reveal types of life evanescing into each other by inexpressible refinements of change.... The faculty for truth is recognised as a power of distinguishing and fixing delicate and fugitive detail. The moral world is ever in contact with the physical, and the relative spirit has invaded moral philosophy from the ground of the inductive sciences. There it has started a new analysis of the relations of body and mind, good and evil, freedom and necessity. Hard and abstract moralities are yielding to a more exact estimate of the subtlety and complexity of life.

Thus the three most perceptive critics of the mid-Victorian period formulated in theoretical terms the problem that confronted the creative writers, and particularly the novelists, in the immediate and empirical form of their methods of telling a story.

From its very beginnings, the English novel claimed to be the supreme vehicle for conveying truth. Defoe, Richardson, Fielding, all insisted that they were honest and conscientious reporters of actuality. Furthermore, each in his own way developed technical procedures to substantiate his claim. Defoe pretended to be merely an editor transmitting autobiographies of existing people to the press. Richardson asserted that by assembling the letters of his protagonists he came even closer to revealing true experience through the chronicle of events as soon as they occurred, uncolored by knowledge of the outcome and retrospective judgment. Fielding preferred the omniscient point of view because thus the inmost meaning of experience could be represented *sub specie aeternitatis.* The novelists of the subsequent half-century followed the same assumptions and employed essentially the same methods.

It was not assumed, of course, that the characters within the story ever knew the full truth, either about their own natures or about the significance of what happened to them. But this limitation did not seriously affect the relationship between the novelist and the reader. Defoe was interested simply in reporting events for their own sake. The modern critics who find multiple significances and ironic implications in *Moll Flanders* are reading meanings into the story that Defoe never intended. Pamela Andrews, Clarissa Harlowe, and Sir Charles Grandison had to maintain a becoming modesty about their own virtues, but there was no question in either Richardson's mind or his reader's as to the merits of these characters or the vices of their adversaries; again it is only the modern critic who analyzes the martyr complex in Clarissa or feels sympathy for Lovelace. The naïveté of Tom Jones is never much mitigated by the crises that beset him, and the novelist makes sure that we shall know the reasons why Tom continues to be an admirable hero in spite of all his misconduct.

The emergence of the *Bildungsroman* marked a realization that truth can be reached only through hard experience, since this is the central theme of every such novel; but the triumphant climax is always the hero's arrival at a mature grasp of reality. Jane Austen is the perfect embodiment of the secure eighteenth-century assumption that common sense is fully adequate for the recognition of truth. The novelist and the reader share the gift of common sense, and jointly enjoy the spectacle of their favorite characters beginning to practice it. When Elizabeth Bennet finally overcomes her prejudice against Darcy, when Emma Woodhouse acknowledges her faulty judgments and her mischievous meddling in other people's lives, even when the ridiculous Catherine Moreland discovers that Northanger Abbey is not a haunt of Gothic horrors, the story is over and the reader is gratified, with no disquieting doubts or uncertainties lurking in shadowy byways of his mind.

Underlying all fiction until the nineteenth century was the unchallenged premise that realism was to be equated with what Ruskin later defined as "imitation." The function of the novelist was that of the reporter, with a subordinate element of accurate description to convey the physical appearance of the characters and the scenery in which they perform. By the close of the eighteenth century, however, potent forces were militating against this view of realism in literature. For the first time the claims of the individual were fully recognized, whether in the political theory of democracy or in the psychological analysis of behavior. If every human being was a unique specimen who, no matter how humble, had a right to express his opinions and to receive equal justice, it was not long until these humanitarian ideals led to the perception that no two people observe alike or evaluate their observations identically, that everybody accepts his own prejudices as facts and feels justified for his actions by his own standards. This revolutionary concept of the multiplicity of truth is as fundamental in all the thinking of the nineteenth century as that of progress was in the thinking of the eighteenth. It profoundly affected the work of every writer, but that of novelists most of all, since they are primarily concerned with the veracious recording and interpreting of experience.

In Victorian fiction—indeed within the work of its most eminent exponent, Dickens—the three successive types of novel can be easily recognized. In his earliest works—*Pickwick, Nicholas Nickleby, Martin Chuzzlewit, The Old Curiosity Shop*—the structure is a simple sequence of events in which the reader feels confident that the author is in firm control of the facts, even though some of them have to be withheld for a while in order to provide suspense and surprise. With equal assurance the reader is aware who are the virtuous characters and who the evil ones, though he may feel an unregenerate affection for those that are both evil and comic, such as Mr Pecksniff or Daniel Quilp. With *David Copperfield* we come to a great *Bildungsroman*, in which the central character gradually and painfully acquires knowledge both of facts and of moral values. It does not take David long to penetrate his aunt's ferocious armor, but years of misjudgment elapse before he reluctantly recognizes that the absurd Tommy Traddles is a person vastly superior to the fascinating Steerforth. It is still, however, a simple matter of one character's growth of comprehension; the reader is not involved in uncertainty as to ultimate values, and indeed usually perceives them sooner than the narrator. In the later novels, on the other hand, the assurance of truth becomes elusive. In *Great Expectations* Pip's elaborate and logical edifice of inference is demolished in the last part of the story, and neither he nor the reader can ever decide whether either the simple-minded Magwitch or the subtle Jaggers is a good character or a bad one. Nor is it ever made clear whether or not Estella loves Pip. In *Bleak House* the camera eye of the omniscient reporter is constantly and disturbingly counterpointed against the innocent and limited observation of Esther Summerson.

A major factor in the new technique was the increasing sophistication of readers. Until the middle of the century, any writer of fiction who hoped for success had to assume that the bulk of his audience was seeking entertainment rather than intellectual challenge. Hence the author felt compelled not only to accept the prevailing ethical standards and social values but also to comment explicitly on the significance of the action and the motivation of the characters. The novel was still struggling to establish itself against lingering Puritan suspicion that fiction was immoral; more importantly, the novel was such a newcomer as a literary genre that even thoroughly literate readers could not be trusted to grasp the full implications of a story without maintaining a firm clutch upon the author's guiding hand. The frequent authorial comments, the overt addresses to the "gentle reader," were not gratuitous intrusions but essential aids to communication.

This condition did not exclude subtlety. Jane Austen, for instance, was a master of implication and irony; but these qualities merely flickered on the surface of her stories, above a solid foundation of assurance in immutable truth. And even Jane Austen, it must be remembered, appealed to only a handful of readers until almost the middle of the century. By that time a few novelists were tentatively beginning to trust that a substantial minority of readers might be able to perceive multiple meanings and oblique suggestions. The maturing of the relationship between writer and reader chanced to coincide with the growing realization that truth was relative and that the old established verities had dissolved into bewildering flux.

The poets, as well as the novelists, were infected by the new uncertainty. For all of them it involved a search for different techniques adequate for embodying the changed attitude in artistically valid forms. Even at the present time their intention is sometimes misunderstood by critics, such as those who condemn Tennyson and Browning for inconsistency or scorn them as muddled thinkers.

One of the primary symptoms of the new uncertainty was distrust of reason and reliance upon intuition as the only medium by which the mind might possibly catch glimpses of some unprovable transcendental truth. This assumption derived in part from the Platonic notion of a higher insight into divine reality, but it differed in significant respects. Even so recent a Platonist as Shelley had taken for granted that reason was a major component in the process by which the state of inspired vision can be achieved. The Victorians, on the contrary, acknowledged that their trust in intuition might be no more than wishful thinking or emotional bias. Arnold could portray Empedocles as uttering a plausibly logical defence of stoic acceptance, with scorn for self-regarding "dreams of future bliss," but the next moment the wise philosopher follows a totally emotional impulse when he leaps into the fiery crater. In a similar poem, Tennyson depicts Lucretius as driven to mania by the conflict between his scientific rationalism and his suppressed passions.

Tennyson's principal method for indicating the fallacy of human reason was not unlike that of dialectical materialism: he presented various incompatible points of view, giving each the benefit of his fluent language and appropriate imagery; and out of the diverse antitheses he tentatively suggested a possible, though unprovable, synthesis. His earliest example, the "Supposed Confessions of a Second-rate Sensitive Mind," is confused and hysterical, and his next one, "The Two Voices," is a mechanical and obvious debate; but "In Memoriam" is a complex review of all the prevalent hypotheses about God and the soul, ranging from scientific rationalism to the oriental belief in reincarnation. Browning's equivalent poem, "Christmas Eve and Easter Day," similarly juxtaposes three utterly unlike schools of thought on religion by describing an evangelical sermon in a London slum, a high mass at St. Peter's in Rome, and a theological lecture in a German university. The two poems both came out in 1850, and in the same year Clough wrote his comparable poem, "Dipsychus," in which the arguments of the Mephistophelian rationalist are more subtle than those of the orthodox believer, and certainly as plausible. One has only to contrast these three poems with Pope's *Essay on Man* to perceive how profound a change had occurred in a hundred and seventeen years.

The most remarkable evidence of the new tone is the emergence of the dramatic monologue as a poetic genre. Tennyson sometimes used it as a method for intensifying his representation of internal confusion. The egotistical young man in "Locksley Hall," and still more the psychotic young man in *Maud*, are buffeted about among antithetical ideas and arrive at conclusions that to most readers are highly questionable. Tennyson emphasized this unreliability when he wrote "Locksley Hall Sixty Years After" and showed the old man qualifying or disavowing many of the prejudices he had expressed in his youth, but uttering equally untenable new prejudices in their stead.

It was Browning, of course, who exploited the full potentialities of the new genre for displaying the relativity of truth. Each speaker of a monologue is convinced of the accuracy of his own knowledge and the validity of his own beliefs. As early as *Sordello*, Browning told his readers that his favorite method was that of

> making speak, myself kept out of view,
> The very man as he was wont to do,
> And leaving you to say the rest for him. . . .
> I should delight in watching first to last
> His progress as you watch it, not a whit
> More in the secret than yourselves. . . .

Browning had to hope that his readers were perceptive enough to realize that the Duke of Ferrara was not actually a magnanimous gentleman who justifiably got rid of an unsatisfactory wife, and that the Bishop of St. Praxed's was not actually a scholarly and saintly prelate who deserved the tribute of a splendid tomb. Not all readers,

then or now, have been sufficiently perspicacious. Even today senti-
mentalists quote Pippa's famous song as an epitome of Browning's
philosophy. The whole point of *Pippa Passes* is the ignorant working
girl's utter misconception of the truth about her fellow residents of
Asolo, and her happy song acquires bitter irony in the context of lust,
greed, and violence. Similarly, several recent scholars have accepted
the illiterate shepherd lad in "Love Among the Ruins" as an author-
ity on ancient history.

Just as *Pippa Passes* was Browning's early dramatization of the
relativity of truth, his eventual masterpiece, *The Ring and the Book*,
is its epic. Each of the nine speakers is positive that he possesses the
vital facts and is competent to interpret them correctly; but not even
the Pope, the wisest and most disinterested of the narrators, achieves
the fullness of knowledge that the reader feels himself to have ac-
quired through absorbing and correlating all the reports. An extra
twist is provided by the second monologue of Guido, proving that
even the same man can offer totally different versions of events, de-
pending on circumstances. Some of Browning's later monologues,
the so-called casuistical ones such as "Bishop Blougram's Apology"
and "Prince Hohenstiel-Schwangau," bewilder naive readers still
more by portraying speakers who are fully aware of the relativity of
truth and with whom the reader partly agrees and partly disagrees as
they subtly discuss their own principles and at the same time betray
their unacknowledged limitations.

The foregoing references to poetry and expository prose have
been necessary in order to display the climate of opinion and the
search for new techniques that environed the novelists of the same
generation. Because authors of prose fiction are not expected to be
so earnestly concerned with philosophic concepts or so scrupulous
about their artistic medium, critics have been tardy in recognizing
that the apparently placid current of their narrative often flowed
over submerged rocks of intellectual originality and was guided into
its channels by cunning artifice.

There is some degree of relationship between the new attitude and
the practice of satire, since the primary object of satire is to make the
reader think for himself and question his previously accepted axi-

oms. But in the novel the relationship is not close. On one hand, two of the major authors most earnestly concerned with the relativity of truth, George Eliot and Henry James, were anything but satirists; on the other, the great satires in fiction, such as *Gulliver's Travels* and *Candide*, can scarcely be included in any valid definition of the novel, since they lack structural complexity, variety of characterization, and illusion of reality, all of which are essentials of the genuine novel. Even such a secondary satirist as Peacock did not create coherent stories or believable characters, but merely offered a series of flat caricature figures, each embodying a single prejudice, and all totally incapable of communicating with one another. The distinction, however, lies much deeper: the satirist is not merely convinced that everyone else is wrong; he is equally positive that he is right, and so his perpetual and obvious intention is to demonstrate his superiority. In contrast, the basic trait of the new outlook is the author's humility in face of Pilate's unanswerable query, "What is truth?"

It was not by satire, therefore, as much as by manipulation of point of view that the new effects were achieved. Neither of the two standard methods, the omniscient or the first-person, was appropriate for indicating all the ironies and intricacies of a relativist view of truth. The most effective device proved to be the onlooker narrator, endowed with neither the limitless knowledge assumed by an omniscient author nor the total recall of a central character recording his experiences. It is this difference in technique, postulating the different concept of truth, that makes *Wuthering Heights* seem immeasurably more modern than *Jane Eyre*. Charlotte Brontë was satisfied with the established autobiographical *Bildungsroman*, in which the narrator conscientiously tells the truth, the whole truth, and nothing but the truth, whereas her sister, by some incalculable flash of insight, enclosed her story in a set of reflecting mirrors. Mr. Lockwood, the complete outsider, is in no position to know any truth of the matter at all. Nelly Dean has had ample opportunity to observe surface phenomena, but is she intelligent enough to interpret what she observes? Professor James Hafley, indeed, has raised the further question as to whether she is even a reliable witness, and ingeniously argues that she is the villain of the tragedy, who distorts every episode in order to justify her behavior. Since the reader is never allowed to enter the mind of any of the principal characters, he remains uninformed about many relevant facts and motives. What was Heathcliff's origin? Why did Mr. Earnshaw adopt him? Was he perhaps Earnshaw's illegitimate son and hence Catherine's half-brother? What was he doing during the years of absence that changed him from a moorland bumpkin to a masterful autocrat? The reader can speculate as he chooses about these mysteries; and the absence of evidence, rather than impairing the book's plausibility, endows it with a convincing effect of the elusiveness and mystery that inhere in our own experience.

The oblique approach to the materials of a story can be seen throughout the fiction of Thackeray. It is largely responsible for the acute differences of opinion that have been advanced by his critics, not only in his own time but at present. In an elementary form it can be seen in his earliest stories, especially the *Yellowplush Papers*, in which the reader is not expected to share the conceited footman's admiration for his scoundrelly master, the Hon. Algernon Percy Deuceace. Thackeray had become more adept by the time he wrote *Barry Lyndon*; and the failure of this story when first published resulted from the reading public's inability to transmute Lyndon's self-righteous boastfulness into the reality of his depravity. It required more than a simple reversal of all values: like many of Browning's monologuists, Lyndon begins to engage the reader's sympathy and win a modicum of admiration. We lose confidence in our ability to decide when he is lying, and we give him credit for merits that are not those he lays claim to.

When Thackeray came to his first full-scale novel, *Vanity Fair*, he had refined his special technique to the point where it was almost imperceptible. Superficially the point of view may appear to be the traditional omniscient one; but gradually one becomes aware that the narrator is an onlooker upon the events, an unidentified but distinctly characterized member of the social circle in which the major figures move, an amiable gossip who picks up and cherishes every detail or rumor that reaches him, but confesses his ignorance at crucial points. In a well-known passage on the responsibility of the novelist, he declares that "one is bound to speak the truth as far as one knows it," and this qualification recurs throughout the book with regard to specific episodes. For example:

> With regard to the world of female fashion and its customs, the present writer can only speak at second hand. A man can no more penetrate or understand those mysteries than he can know what the ladies talk about when they go upstairs after dinner. It is only by inquiry and perseverance that one sometimes gets hints of those secrets; and by a similar diligence every person who treads the Pall Mall pavement and frequents the clubs of this metropolis, knows, either through his own experience or through some acquaintance with whom he plays at billiards or shares the joint, something about the genteel world of London. . . . (Ch. 37)

Again: "As I cannot describe the mysteries of freemasonry, although I have a shrewd idea that it is a humbug; so an uninitiated man cannot take upon himself to portray the great world accurately, and had best keep his opinions to himself whatever they are." (Ch. 51) From the evidence presented, the reader will certainly infer that Becky was Lord Steyne's mistress, and that she murdered Jos Sedley; but the narrator is not in a position to certify these slanderous implications and so he is scrupulous to avoid stating them.

Later, in *The Newcomes*, Thackeray undertook a further experiment. The bystander-narrator in this book is a clearly identified individual, a friend of the hero and an occasional minor participant in the occurrences; but also he is Arthur Pendennis, who had been the central figure in a previous novel. Thus one work of fiction is presented through the intermediacy of a fictitious character established in another, and the omniscient author somehow vanishes in the process.

George Eliot ostensibly remained faithful to the convention of the author's unlimited knowledge; but her most noted pronouncement, in *Adam Bede*, is as cautious as Thackeray's was:

> My strongest effort . . . is to give a faithful account of men and things as they have mirrored themselves in my mind. The mirror is doubtless defective; the outlines will sometimes be dis-

turbed, the reflection faint or confused; but I feel as much bound to tell you as precisely as I can what the reflection is, as if I were in the witness-box narrating my experience on oath. (Ch. 17)

Later she remarks again: "I believe the wisest of us must be beguiled ... sometimes, and must think both better and worse of people than they deserve. Nature has her language, and she is not unveracious; but we don't know all the intricacies of her syntax just yet, and in a hasty reading we may happen to extract the very opposite of her real meaning." (Ch. 25).

In her narrative technique, moreover, sometimes George Eliot unobtrusively adopted the new principle of uncertainty. The key scene of Hetty's seduction is conveyed solely through an apparently trivial action by Arthur Donnithorne, when he is alone in the summerhouse after his fight with Adam: "He went cautiously round the room as if wishing to assure himself of the presence or absence of something. At last he had found a slight thing, which he put first in his pocket, and then, on a second thought, took out again, and thrust deep down into a waste-paper basket. It was a woman's little pink silk neckerchief." Subsequently, the reader is not explicitly told what happened to Hetty's baby. Was it born alive or dead? Did she kill it, or abandon it? As a basis for our inferences, we are given an account of her disturbed state of mind before the birth, and later the incriminating evidence as formally presented at the trial. But actually we know no more about what happened than the spectators in a courtroom can ever know. As there were no witnesses to the event, only Hetty could have reported the facts; and her disturbed condition precluded even her as a reliable source of information.

As the antithesis of this situation, wherein nobody can claim to know the truth, there is the more frequent one in which too many people are confident that they know it, and yet no two agree. This theme was satirically emphasized by Browning in *The Ring and the Book* through the three rank outsiders, "One Half Rome," "The Other Half Rome," and "Tertium Quid." Meredith uses extraneous and cocksure observers in the extracts from the memoirs of Henry Wilmers and Perry Wilkinson at the beginning of *Diana of the*

Crossways, and in the voice of Dame Gossip throughout *The Amazing Marriage*. George Eliot manipulates the huge cast of characters in *Middlemarch* to achieve a comparable effect. Almost every episode —the hospital controversy, the Bulstrode scandal, the marital troubles of the Lydgates—being filtered to us through the minds and feelings of the participants, is colored by their temperaments; and also recurrently the uninformed outsiders make themselves heard in voices of gossip or ridicule, intolerance or misplaced sympathy. A similar effect was produced by Trollope in *The Warden*, when the whole community of Barchester, and later the London press, become involved in the dispute over Hiram's Hospital. John Bold, Archdeacon Grantly, the pensioners, the editor of *The Jupiter*, the leaders of public opinion represented by Dr Pessimist Anticant and Mr Popular Sentiment, all feel positive that they understand the full meaning of Hiram's bequest and the proper way of implementing or revising it. Only the character most concerned, Mr. Harding, admits to uncertainty, and the conflicting interpretations offered by the others reduce him to bewilderment. At the end nobody has been rewarded or punished or even persuaded to change one iota of his opinions. Poor harried Mr. Harding has taken a step that satisfies none of the opposing parties and probably leaves every reader doubtful whether to approve it. If the story arrives at any conclusion, it is that all the diverse views on the problem are equally valid, and none has any validity beyond what its exponent can establish by sheer audacity.

Just as important as the technical matter of point of view, and just as likely to baffle unwary readers, is the question of the author's attitude. Here again Thackeray is the first noteworthy example. Many of his contemporaries detested him as a dastardly cynic. Many critics at the present day sneer at him as a syrupy sentimentalist. The divergence of opinion extends also to his feelings toward his characters. Does he approve or disapprove of Becky Sharp? Does he like or dislike Amelia Sedley? Does he think that William Dobbin is wise or foolish? The proper answer to all such questions is simply "yes." Whether Dobbin is wise or foolish depends on each reader's judgment, and usually he is both at once. We can be fond of Amelia even while she exasperates us; we can admire Becky's intelligence and courage even if we abhor her lack of scruple. Cynicism and sentimentality are merely two ways of looking at evidence in search of the truth that underlies it. A consistently cynical novel would be as heinously false as a consistently sentimental one. Only by a perpetual interplay between the two, an amalgam of disillusioned common sense and irrational sympathy, is there any route toward even a minimum of insight into the inscrutable reality.

George Meredith went much further in employing the shifting lights of inconsistent attitudes. *The Ordeal of Richard Feverel* has equal proportions of romantic tragedy and satiric comedy, of poetic extravagance and realistic precision. The selfish, sensual Adrian Harley is the most despicable character in the book, and yet many of his malicious epigrams strike the reader as disturbingly true. Sir Austin Feverel is a monomaniac who shares with Adrian the responsibility for the catastrophes in the story, but again and again his aphorisms embody ideas that Meredith firmly believed in. Even muddle-headed Mrs Berry often penetrates closer to the elusive truth than do the more rational characters, and she utters several of the most astute comments in the book.

A further way of casting varicolored lights upon the narrative was by fluctuation of style. Mock-heroic grandiloquence, burlesque, or outright parody could reveal the absurdity of conventional literary representations of experience. In the first edition of *Vanity Fair*, chapter six included specimens of how the story might have been handled by writers of the Newgate and the Silver-fork schools. Trollope parodied Carlyle and Dickens in the articles by Dr Anticant and Mr Sentiment, in *The Warden*. Meredith lapsed frequently into parody, but more briefly and less explicitly. In chapter 23 of *The Egoist*, Sir Willoughby Patterne imagines a parting interview with Clara in what Meredith calls "the language of the imaginative composition of his time, favorite readings in which had inspired Sir Willoughby with a colloquy so pathetic." He envisions Clara talking like this: "We part. In mercy let it be forever. Oh, terrible word! Coined by the passions of our youth, it comes to us for our sole riches when we are bankrupt of earthly treasures, and is the passport given by Abnegation unto Woe that prays to quit this probationary sphere. . . ."

Meredith ventured far beyond Thackeray and George Eliot also in the condensation or omission of whole scenes or items of information that the simple rules of factual narrative would regard as obligatory. Sometimes, as with Sir Willoughby's climactic humiliation in *The Egoist*, the author openly avows that he has no intention of representing the scene; elsewhere, as with Robert Armstrong's attack on Edward Blancove in *Rhoda Fleming*, and Dahlia's wedding in the same novel, he tacitly ignores the event when it occurs and later drops casual clues by which it can be reconstructed. Many critics have scoffed at this habit as sheer incompetence in narration or as timid evasion of difficult episodes; but it can be regarded also as a deliberate device for suggesting the relativity of truth by shifting the normal proportion and emphasis in much the same way as modern painters distort visual reality in favor of subjective significance.

Omission or under-emphasis, like parody, helped to impugn the accepted standards of demonstrable truth. A notable example is Thackeray's presentation of the Battle of Waterloo through the terror and suspense and fortitude of various characters in Brussels, miles from the scene of action. Not only is Thackeray avoiding the pretentious set pieces of the standard historical novel; he is also discounting the assumption of professional historians that in presenting the whole truth about momentous events they need concentrate solely upon battlefields and parliamentary crises. Early in the novel he had remarked, "Are there not little chapters in everybody's life, that seem to be nothing, and yet affect all the rest of the history?" In the Waterloo episode he implies that this principle prevails in world affairs as well as in individual careers.

In Meredith's novels it is sometimes not an episode but a character that is under-emphasized to the verge of invisibility. Clare Forey in *Richard Feverel* remains a shadowy figure in the background until after her death, when her diary reveals her tragic personality and her involvement in preceding events. If Richard had been the narrator or the focal intelligence of the whole novel, this would have been natural enough; but as the point of view is ostensibly omniscient, the device can be recognized as Meredith's method of conveying the indefinable truth of Clare's self-effacing personality.

In this instance the reader is permitted, though belatedly, to learn the relevant facts. Sometimes, however, Meredith never supplies positive information on what seems to be a vital matter. The whole action of *Harry Richmond* hinges upon Richmond Roy's claim to be of royal blood, but we remain in the dark as to whether the claim was true or false and—if false—whether he believed it himself or was a calculating impostor. For the essential purpose of the story, however, elucidation is not needed. Roy's impact upon his son and everyone else within his orbit remains the same; and documentary proof, one way or the other, would merely be a concession to the literal-minded reader who identifies truth with specific facts.

Examples could be multiplied from the novels of the mid-century. We cannot here touch upon another manifestation of the new approach, which Ruskin mentioned in his perceptive remark that "Truth may be stated by any signs or symbols which have a definite signification in the minds of those to whom they are addressed, although such signs be themselves no image nor likeness of anything." Only in recent years have critics of the novel begun to catch up with Ruskin in recognizing the importance of symbolism in fiction as a vehicle for the communication of truth.

It has not been my purpose to argue that the new kind of fiction was aesthetically or morally or intellectually superior to any that preceded it. I have intended rather to demonstrate that an influential new concept, which invaded every sphere of human thinking near the middle of the nineteenth century, was bound to affect the methods, the materials, and the attitudes of the novelists. They stand as transitional figures between the confidence in objective fact that characterized the age of reason and the unabashed solipsism that came into fiction in the present century through the stream-of-consciousness technique.

FLOYD B. LAWRENCE

Lyric and Romance: Meredith's Poetic Fiction

T HERE HAVE BEEN many attempts to systematize the ways in which critics might estimate the relative merits of novelists. One of the most productive originates in this question: how has the artist managed to meet the essential requirement of all fiction—the telling of an "interesting" story, as James observed— in a truly original or, as it were, novel fashion? There are perhaps as many different answers to this question as there are novelists. We each have our pat answers whenever Richardson, Miss Austen, Dickens, or Joyce happens to occupy our attention. The following remarks on George Meredith's fiction are intended to make less pat our response to his work, especially as it is represented in his first and last novels: *The Ordeal of Richard Feverel* (1859) and *The Amazing Marriage* (1895). I should like to forego the customary task of determining Meredith's success in comic fiction in favor of some attempt to examine and evaluate the peculiarly poetic themes and techniques which appear in these books. By the term "poetic" I mean quite simply that embellishment of the bare bones of the story which borrows from the traditional prerogatives of the poet, in the strict sense of the term. In particular, I wish to point out the ways in which Meredith employed some of the techniques of the lyric and the poetic romance.

I make no claim that such embellishment of fiction is unique with Meredith; I do claim, however, that my subject is one which has long been recognized but never, in Meredith's case, sufficiently analyzed. Certain dangers of distortion always exist whenever traditional distinctions between genres are not fully respected—when the same critical vocabulary is used, for instance, to discuss a lyric poem and a prose epic. Nevertheless I believe that ample precedent for such procedure exists in the work of such critics as Joseph Frank, Donald Stauffer, Northrop Frye, and Kenneth Burke, to name but a few.[1] Especially to be avoided is the occasional tendency to make one's own critical errors or shortcomings look like creative blunders of the artist under discussion. I have tried to avoid this temptation.

It is infrequently noted that the subtitle of *The Ordeal of Richard Feverel* is "A History of Father and Son." Now ordinarily a "history of" anything in the context of title or subtitle conditioned the novel readers of the eighteenth and nineteenth centuries to large doses of detailed exposition and concrete description, especially during the early chapters dealing with genealogy, money, physical scene, or some combination of these. In the first edition of *Feverel*, Meredith strove to meet his readers' expectations by filling them in on the "quiescent Tories" who comprise Sir Austin Feverel's ancestors, by sketching in the circumstances surrounding Lady Feverel's jilting of her husband, and by showing the descent of the curse of the Ordeal through the house of Feverel. Meredith chose to delete much of this when he condensed the first four chapters into one for the 1878 edition. Whether he was unwilling or unable to treat ordinary exposition with ordinary assurance and proportion is a difficult question to answer. In any case, the difference between adequate and inadequate handling of this task in fiction might become apparent in a brief comparison of two passages—one by Meredith and one by Dickens—the purpose of which is to describe physical setting. The first passage is from *Richard Feverel* and concerns the ancestral house of the Feverels, Raynham Abbey:

> The house they lived in, called an Abbey from some tradition of its site, was a heterogeneous architectural jumble, which nevertheless presented a generous front to a broad westward valley of green pastures, fruitful tillage, and a pure-flowing wave; and seen from the river, on its platform of greensward, backed by lofty pines and flanked with beechwoods midway down a hillocky roll of grass, that ended in flat rich meadows

extending to the river-side, deserved some better title than that
of Raynham Ramshackle, as the Papworths, old political an-
tagonists of the Feverels, delighted to term it.[2]

The second selection comes from Chapter Three of *Dombey and
Son*:

> Mr. Dombey's house was a large one, on the shady side of a
> tall, dark, dreadfully genteel street in the region between Port-
> land Place and Bryanstone Square. It was a corner house, with
> great wide areas containing cellars frowned upon by barred
> windows, and leered at by crooked-eyed doors leading to dust-
> bins. It was a house of dismal state, with a circular back to it,
> containing a whole suit of drawing-rooms looking upon a grav-
> elled yard, where two gaunt trees, with blackened trunks and
> branches, rattled rather than rustled, their leaves were so
> smoke-dried.[3]

Though Meredith does tell us elsewhere that the "river-side" in the
Feverel passage is that of the Thames, he does very little else to place
the reader in time or space or to orient him to the actual seat of the
Feverels. With Dickens the case is much different. Here we are at a
particular corner at a well-defined dwelling; what is more, we are
temporally placed in a time of increasing industrialism, a feat which
is obliquely achieved by the narrator's obvious attitude toward the
obnoxious "smoke-dried" leaves on the "two gaunt trees." Meredith's "lofty pines" and "beechwoods," on the other hand, convey little more than an image of grandeur, ironically qualified by the opposite judgment of the Papworths, who play virtually no role at all in
the novel. The Dickensian activity of such verbs as "frowned upon,"
"leered," and "rattled," is quite unlike the pictorial passivity of
Meredith's "presented" and "flanked." As an example of what Kenneth Burke has called "factional" technique, the passage from Dickens is the more successful of the two.

Other attempts to "fill the reader in," so to speak, are made
through the character of Adrian Harley, an early experiment in the
voice of comic wit. But the reader fails to be convinced by much that
Adrian says, for two reasons: his cynical frigidity toward the other
characters in the novel makes him morally reprehensible, and, more

importantly, his role of poseur makes most of his remarks on the world of the "social gods" seem completely gratuitous. Since Meredith did give so much attention to Adrian, and since Adrian's influence in the novel is so limited, we can conclude that Meredith felt both the desirability and the difficulty of sketching in the staples of the novel as "history of" something or as social comedy in the vein of Jane Austen or Thackeray.

It is my contention, then, that a reading of the novel which emphasizes almost exclusively the social or didactic themes places the emphasis on the weakest and most uncertain parts of the book. Thus, if we are primarily interested in what Meredith thought about, say, the new educational theories of Herbert Spencer, or the increasing numbers of London streetwalkers at mid-century, or the abuses of Tory landholders during the same period, we shall not be satisfied with what we find in *Richard Feverel*. Of course these and many related topics in the novel may prove to be nourishing to the literary historian who is hungry for footnotes. But, speaking from the point of view of the literary critic, my concern is with the often neglected element of lyricism in the text which gives it its special appeal.

It is, I believe, significant that Frederick Karl has observed "a falling off, a weakening of the forward thrust of the novel" in the final third of *Feverel*, since this is precisely the most factional section and contains most of the undiluted social comedy.[4] Professor Karl is merely the most recent critic to express a dissatisfaction with this section. It is indeed painfully obvious that Meredith's pen was not up to the task of drawing a satisfying backdrop for Richard's adventures in the sophisticated and urban world of the city, away from the isolated rusticity of Raynham Abbey. And it would be easiest to account for this by pointing out that this is, after all, a first novel, and that good social comedy demands an experienced imagination. Up to a certain point, such an explanation is acceptable. Such negative observations, however, fail to define the specific positive excellences of the earlier, lyric portions of the novel, those portions which, to use Burke's terminology again, are universalized rather than factional. Since this task of definition presents itself, my remaining remarks on *Feverel* will be directed toward that end.

Given modern experiments in lyric prose, such as those found in Lawrence, Joyce, and Virginia Woolf, it is a tendency for the literary historian or critic to look back upon earlier, and therefore clumsier, Victorian attempts at such writing with a mixture of scorn and condescension. David Daiches, for example, speaks admiringly of D. H. Lawrence's "lyrical feeling for the creative rhythms underlying all genuine experience," and hastens to add that in a Lawrence novel we find something more than "highfalutin 'poetic' prose of a kind we are accustomed to in the Victorian novel."[5] Daiches does not mention Meredith in his sweeping statement; but with something of the same attitude, Walter F. Wright says of *Richard Feverel*: "The ornamental framework of the novel possesses a certain charm, though one would prefer a more Doric simplicity . . . ."[6] And Lionel Stevenson, though he acknowledges the "glowing imagery" and "rhythmic movement" of many of the descriptive passages, concludes that the book is essentially "an extended personal essay in the guise of fiction."[7] Because of her own creative propensities, it is only natural that Virginia Woolf should have admired the lyrical episodes in Meredith's fiction, which she did in an essay in *The Common Reader*.[8] Despite Mrs. Woolf's admiration and the frequent admiration of many students of *Feverel*, the effect and meaning of Meredith's lyricism remain essentially undefined.

The lyrical touchstone in the first half of the novel is, of course, Chapter 18, "Ferdinand and Miranda." The magical quality of *The Tempest* is immediately invoked with the chapter title. We are told at the outset, furthermore, that "Raynham hung in mists, remote . . . ." The universalized nature of the setting is thus assured. Also contributing to the lyrical quality are the many images of musicality frequently woven into the texture of the writing: Lucy speaks "musically," and a "sweet Heaven-bird" shivers out his song above Richard. But even more significantly musical is the way in which the normal progress of the narrative is greatly suspended, almost in the manner of a climactic chord. Richard's perception of Lucy, described in the following passage from the end of Chapter 17, forms the apex of the lyrical moment of stasis:

Surrounded by the green shaven meadows, the pastoral summer buzz, the weir-fall's thundering white, amid the breath and beauty of wildflowers, she was a bit of lovely human life in a fair setting—a terrible attraction. The Magnetic Youth leaned round to note his proximity to the weir-piles, and beheld the sweet vision. Stiller and stiller grew Nature, as at the meeting of two electric clouds. Her posture was so graceful that, though he was making straight for the weir, he dared not dip a scull. (p. 120)

The impression is not of a story being told but of a moment of universal harmony between man and his natural environment being caught, almost frozen, in all its facets. Blackbirds sing, kingfishers flash, herons are aroused, Lucy's curls become one in color with the shafts of sunlight, her lips are stained with dewberries, and, most important, the very meeting of Richard and Lucy strikes us as a most natural and credible incident, inevitable in the plan of nature.

The meeting of Ferdinand and Miranda, in other words, does not smack of mere coincidence. In addition to portraying the lovers as part of the natural scheme of things, Meredith prepares the psychological ground for the meeting with great care and skill. And he does this with a method which is quite common to the lyric artist: he deliberately blurs the edges of the world of dream and the world of reality. For instance, in Chapter 17, called "An Attraction," we find Richard in bed dreaming wildly in romantic terms of "knights and ladies" and especially of one pair of ladies' eyes, and of "a hand glittering white and fragrant as the frosted blossom of a May-night" (p. 115). Needless to say, the eyes and the white hand of Richard's dream are concretely realized in Chapter 18 during the waking dream which comprises the actual encounter with Miranda. A similar incident occurs as early as Chapter Three when a secret and surprise nocturnal visit on the part of Lady Feverel is preceded by Richard's dream of "a beautiful lady! beautifuller than my Nurse . . ." (p. 18). Looking back in literary history, one is reminded of what Wordsworth called "one of those sweet dreams" which invariably merges with actual experience; looking forward, one might make some comparison between Richard's visions and those of Joyce's Dedalus. The essentially lyrical impulse to realize dream vision through tangible objects of experience exists strongly in each case. With this in mind, we can understand a narrative remark made shortly after the marriage of the young lovers: "Lucy awoke from dreams which seemed reality, to the reality which was a dream." (p. 257) Unquestionably Lucy is modelled after the innocent pastoral beauty of Meredith's 1851 poem, "Love in the Valley," who is found in the first stanza dreaming under a beech tree.[9]

In addition, Richard's lyric indulgence in dreams relates to his impulses to write poetry, to give form to his experience, as we see in the following passage:

> . . . chaotic hosts, like ranks of stormy billows, pressed impetuously for expression, and despair of reducing them to form, quite as much as pride, to which it pleased him to refer his incapacity, threw down the powerless pen, and sent him panting to his outstretched length and another headlong career through the rosy-girdled land. (p. 115)

The form-giving experience with Lucy does not, however, totally satisfy Richard, especially when his dreams get so out of hand that he feels compelled to reform the world. The search for form goes on in the later portions of the novel and is the controlling factor in Richard's vulnerability to the inflammatory Judith Felle. "Richard felt his safety," we learn, "in this which, to please the world, we must term Folly. Exhalation of vapours was a wholesome process to him, and somebody who gave them shape and hue a beneficent Iris. He told Austin plainly he could not leave her, and did not anticipate the day when he could." (p. 443)

Judging from the uneven quality of the novel—the formally superior lyrical portions of the earlier sections and the unsteady narrative of the later social comedy—it would appear that in his own act of composition, Meredith faced problems of form which oddly resembled the problems of his protagonist. The isolated pastoral world of the Abbey, and, later, the wilderness of the Rhineland apparently supplied workable materials with which to develop the themes of young love and personal responsibility. The variegated worlds of London or Richmond, on the other hand, provided at best settings for analogous themes of enchantment and duty. What must be observed is that the lyrical portions of the novel comprise, almost by themselves, the primary substance of the novel's plot, characterization, and theme. Love, pride, organic development, duty, idealism—all of these and more are treated with assurance in one or another of the many lyrical interludes. The flames of the burning rick, for example, provide a symbolic equation for Richard's passionate assertion of self in the face of more mundane demands. Similar probing of the hero's unconscious appears in the striking scene when Richard observes Lady Blandish's bonnet at the swimming match and is, quite literally, frozen in his tracks. There is more of an affinity between such scenes and, for instance, Joyce's epiphanies than has previously been recognized. Against such writing, it is easier to see why the lyrical hero out of his lyrical element is portrayed in terms which are weakly duplicative or are formally confusing.

The disparate nature of *Richard Feverel* is, of course, not as obvious as it may sound from the foregoing discussion, since constant attempts are made to stitch together the universal with the factional, the lyrical with the comic, and the voice of sensibility with the voice of wit. But the artistic surgery in this early effort is much too clumsy for the discriminating reader. Consequently Virginia Woolf can say with good reason that after Meredith's narrator finishes his lyrical song, the characters frequently "move again with a jerk."[10] But Kenneth Burke offers what I think is the most incisive statement about the lyrical artist who is confronted with the problem of having to write in ways which are not always strictly lyrical. Although the following excerpt contains some terms used in dramatic criticism, the point emphasized lends support to Professor Karl's remarks about the falling off of *Richard Feverel* in the later stages:

> ... imagine a 'lyric' plot that had reduced the intrigue business to a minimum. When the poet had completed Act III, his job would be ended, and despite his intention to write a work in five acts, he might very well feel a loss of inclination to continue into Acts IV and V. For the act of foreshadowing, in Act III, would already *implicitly contain* the culmination of the promises. ... Hence, it would *serve as surrogate* for the *quality* with which he had intended to end Act V, whereat the poet

would have no good reason to continue further. He would 'lose interest'—and precisely because the quality of Act V had been 'telescoped' into the quality of Act III that foreshadowed it . . . . Act III would be a kind of ejaculation too soon, with the purpose of the composition forthwith dwindling.[11]

In other words, we might say with reference to *Richard Feverel* that no amount of intrigue or social comedy in the later stages of the novel can either generate or sustain the intense responses called up by the earlier lyrical sections. Meredith's readers, for example, can recognize in the lyric passages the course that Richard's subsequent adventures will take, so that much of the later intrigue simply becomes needless duplication. In this sense Meredith may be accused of structural mishandling, and presumably some awareness of the difficulties created thereby may have been in his mind as he revised the novel for later editions.

Finally, some acknowledgment must be made of the controversial ending of the novel. This then is the old question for feverish admirers of *Feverel*: is Lucy's death an arbitrary incident which buys tragedy at the expense of consistency or credibility? Can the reader agree with J. B. Priestley's opinion that "*Richard Feverel* is presented as a comedy, and has a tragic ending thrust upon it, quite arbitrarily"?[12] Must we agree with the critic who recently analyzed the book by searching for principles of comic structure and who prefaced his search with the judgment that the ending of the novel is "formally inappropriate"?[13] I think that a careful and tolerant reading shows that we need not agree with such observations, and that some defense of the ending can be made once we have comprehended the foregoing distinctions.

Nowhere does Lucy Desborough strike us as typical of the heroines of much contemporary Victorian fiction, namely the sort of girl who must suffer tragically if she has had some hand in helping the hero sow his wild oats. The reaction of the *Westminster Review*, however, is typical of those who look for such social lessons in the pages of *Feverel*: "What of the sowing of wild oats of which the novelist has so much to say?" the reviewer asks. "Are they to be sown or not, those wild oats? We do not feel that we are brought

any nearer by the experience of Richard Feverel to the solution of
that great social question about the sowing of wild oats."[14] But
neither Lucy nor the event of Lucy's death was designed to promote
discussion of social questions. Lucy, we must remember, belongs
almost completely to that lyrical, youthful world in which dream
and reality tend to merge. As such, she stays, for the most part, on a
highly symbolic level. Her identification with the Virgin in Chapter
46 serves to enhance her function as universalized symbol. Her inno-
cence, generosity, genuine passion, and wholesale devotion to Richard can remain viable virtues only if she is not violated by being
brought into the antithetical world of the factional. Such a viola-
tion does in fact occur, and the result can only spell her doom, both
as a character and as a literary device. One way in which she is
brought into the precarious real world is, of course, by virtue of her
marriage to Richard, who feels a mad compulsion to straddle both
worlds.

But in addition to Lucy's marriage and the obvious symbol of the
cypress tree, Meredith offers subtler but stronger evidence for the
inevitability of Lucy's fate. Near the end of the novel, Lord Mountfalcon busily engages in a scheme to seduce Lucy, and Lucy, unaware
of his sinister intentions, instinctively forestalls any real advances
by having the aristocrat read to her during the evenings when Richard is away with Judith Felle. The reading assumes a metaphoric
role, as we see in the following key scene:

> When they were alone again, Lucy said, smiling, "Do you
> know, I am always ashamed to ask you to begin to read."
> Mountfalcon stared. "To read?—oh! ha! yes!" he remem-
> bered his evening duties. "Very happy, I'm sure. Let me see.
> Where were we?"
> "The life of the Emperor Julian. But indeed I feel quite
> ashamed to ask you to read, my lord. It's too new to me—like a
> new world—hearing about Emperors, and armies, and things
> that really have been on the earth we walk upon. It fills my
> mind." (p. 404)

It is not a distortion of the text to say that the reading itself is a
form of Mountfalcon's seduction and that a rape of the mind ensues

when Lucy's affinity with the pastoral is terminated by even a secondhand introduction to "Emperors, and armies, and things. . . ."
Her death is only the literal manifestation of the death of the lyrical
impulse in the novel. It is really neither tragic nor comic, but simply
an inevitable fact of existence which no amount of Sir Austin's
scientific planning can prevent. It is the greatest ordeal that must
be endured. As the harsh voice of Nature says in *Modern Love*:
"I play for Seasons; not Eternities!" And, if we read the last few
sentences of the Ferdinand-Miranda chapter carefully enough, we
find that Richard's loss is amply prefigured there:

> ... away with her went the wild enchantment ... Tomorrow
> this spot will have a memory—the river, and the meadow, and
> the white, falling weir; his heart will build a temple here, and
> the skylark will be its high-priest, and the old blackbird its
> glossy-gowned chorister, and there will be a sacred repast of
> dewberries. (pp. 127-28)

The moment of lyric enchantment, the narrator seems to be telling
us here and in the structure of the story as a whole, is both fleeting
and permanent. When such moments are enshrined in art through
memory, when, that is, they are treated lyrically, as they are in this
novel, they acquire their sole claim to permanence.

It is safe to conclude then that *The Ordeal of Richard Feverel*
is, after all, a form of the novel as history; but the sort of history
which concerns Meredith resembles the psychological history of the
modern novelist more than the factional history of many of Meredith's predecessors and contemporaries. History in *Feverel* consists
of the progress of a mind from its early exalted lyric enchantment,
through its quest to derive order from that enchanted experience,
through its dependence on memory for self-renewal, and concluding
in the shock of disenchantment or, in the history of Sir Austin Feverel, morbid withdrawal.

It has often been noted that, paradoxically, Meredith's own self
appears in both Sir Austin and Richard; so we might at least tentatively conclude that this history of father and son can be more
coherently viewed as the history of one mind—Meredith's own.
And such a reading, though for the most part beyond my present

scope, would give the novel an even deeper dimension of lyric involvement.

In my discussion of *Richard Feverel*, I have neglected to mention the most salient "poeticizing" which Meredith used: the frequent metaphoric embellishment achieved through repeated allusions to the form and substance of traditional ballad and romance.[15] For the most part, the irony achieved through such writing is apparent. From his slaying of the dragon in the person of Heavy Benson to his chivalric intention to slay all the social dragons in sight, Richard's exalted notions of himself provide a major part of the comic criticism which Meredith obviously intended in the novel.

In his last completed novel, *The Amazing Marriage*, published in 1895 but begun at least twelve years before,[16] Meredith turned to the conventions of the ballad and romance to fashion a highly complex narrative framework which reveals much about his own tastes in storytelling. The relatively simple irony of *Richard Feverel* is replaced in this book by a much more sympathetic concern with the stock elements of romance: extravagance, heavy emphasis on action and episode, and characters motivated in an intense, almost monomaniacal, way. The title itself, perhaps Meredith's most extravagant since *The Shaving of Shagpat*, is an adequate first clue to some of the dizzying movement in the book.

Since *The Amazing Marriage* is one of the least known novels in Meredith's canon, perhaps a very brief description of narrative structure would clarify the critical discussion. The first three chapters are narrated by a persona whom Meredith chose to call Dame Gossip, who plays a highly important role throughout the rest of the novel as well. To her falls the task of describing the initial amazing marriage, that between Captain John Peter Avason Kirby, a descendent of the "Danish rovers" nearing his seventieth year, and the Countess of Cresset, nicknamed in the popular ballads of the time the Countess Fanny, a twenty-three year old Irish girl whose first marriage to Lord Cresset is a millstone around her spirited neck. With great flair, Captain Kirby steals Fanny from under the lord's nose at midnight on the twenty-first of June. Lord Cresset soon dies;

the Captain and the Countess are married in Switzerland; their first child is named Chillon Switzer John Kirby; and, after the parents move to Austria, they have a daughter named Carinthia Jane, the heroine of the novel, who is named after the Austrian province. Chillon is sent to England to work with his uncle, Lord Levellier, in the development of new explosives, and the separation from his worried mother brings about the Countess Fanny's death. In good Heathcliffian fashion, Captain Kirby dies a week later in a remote mountain forest.

With the beginning of Chapter IV, Chillon returns for his sister, and the Meredithian narrator takes over to describe their departure from the mountain home to the world below. These opening chapters strikingly resemble the historical romances of the first half of the century; complex explanations of genealogy and geography overwhelm the reader. Even more pervasive is Dame Gossip's nostalgia for an age which has since dwindled in color and vibrancy. Repeatedly, after describing a near-miraculous occurrence, she confides to the reader: "You know what those days were," or "Such days those were!" Relying mainly on popular ballads as her sources, she knows little and cares less about the motives her characters have for acting as they do. "I give it you as it stands here printed," she warns the reader; "I do not profess to understand."[17] In short, she is quite unlike the typical Meredithian narrator, even the narrator in the opening pages of *Diana of the Crossways,* who was similarly concerned with providing an historical framework for his story. Her sole concern seems to be to capture what Professor Stevenson has described as "the very spirit of the Regency-Byronic period."[18]

Most observers of the novel, and they are not overly numerous, dismiss by implication the Dame's function to that of a mere antinarrator, a kind of fickle and indulgent old lady who could not and would not subscribe to a new brand of storytelling that sacrificed the adventurous verve of popular songs, ballads, or romances. In many ways, she is thus the perfect antithesis of Meredith's more conventional narrative voice; and the running warfare between the two narrators in the novel substantiates this claim. Dame Gossip despises narrative psychologizing which is "designed for a frequent arrest of the actors in the story and a searching of the internal state of this one or that one of them. . . ." In one of her frequent "irruptions," as they are called in Chapter XIII, she makes her preferences quite clear:

> Now, as it is good for those to tell who intend preserving their taste for romance and hate anatomical lectures, we never can come to the exact motives of any extraordinary piece of conduct on the part of man or woman. . . . I say we must with due submission accept the facts. We are not a bit the worse for wondering at them. (p. 177)

The conventional narrator, on the other hand, chastises the Dame— "in her vagrant fowl's treatment of a story . . . she may ultimately addle"—for neglecting to mention small but significant details of the action which may be extremely revealing.

Given such a dichotomy in the narrative structure of *The Amazing Marriage*, we are bound to interpret the excessive title and the Dame's function in the novel ironically. The Dame becomes nothing but an elaborately drawn scapegoat who embodies all of the fictional techniques which, presumably, Meredith himself had already forsaken in his quest for a more psychological fiction with a much more private appeal.[19] To use the handy terms devised by Northrop Frye, we might say that Meredith's intent in this novel was to swing the fictional pendulum away from the modes of romance and high mimetic toward those of low mimetic and irony.[20] To do so effectively, we might assume, he would have had to rely less on a portrayal of the marvelous and the superior in his characters, and more on an exposure of their essential humanity, including their many foibles. Like Thackeray, he would write a novel which for all purposes was without a hero. In addition, as a way of supplying an artistic foil to the cantankerous Dame, he would reduce his emphasis on story, or mere action, and devote more time to acute probing of the consciousness of his characters.

Such a description of Meredith's technique is, I feel, appropriate to describe much of his work, especially *The Egoist*, where not even the indomitable Clara Middleton and Vernon Whitford are spared some gentle scourging by the Comic Spirit. However, a careful reading of *The Amazing Marriage* reveals that Meredith's purpose in this instance was not merely a simple comic subversion of the excesses of romance; rather we find that after the initial task of subversion is completed, Meredith actually succeeds in constructing a new romance comprised of some of the very things which Dame Gossip feels have disappeared along with Byron, ballads, and the Regency. In the following observations, I hope to show how and why Meredith took such a task upon himself.

The ostensible hero of the story is Edward Russett, the Earl of Fleetwood, who might best be described as Sir Willoughby Patterne with spurs on. He is indescribably wealthy and can for this reason afford to exclude if not scorn the world in a manner that Willoughby cannot. But even more perplexing to those who know him, and to the reader, is the absolute arbitrariness of much of his behavior. His fantastic notions of personal honor, for instance, lead him to keep his word on all occasions; thus, when he impulsively proposes marriage to Carinthia, he must marry her, despite his aversion to her roughly hewn surface. Immediately after the marriage, he sweeps Carinthia off to witness a boxing match. Sometime later, the reader learns with some bewilderment that Carinthia has given birth to Lord Fleetwood's child. But only after this fact is given do we learn that Fleetwood's aversion to Carinthia was not total, for on their wedding night he impulsively visits her by climbing a ladder to the window of her room at the inn where he had earlier deposited her. Many readers of the novel have objected to this rather crude postponement of information on Meredith's part. But the humor and mystery surrounding the honeymoon stimulate the reader's guesswork and thereby heighten the desired atmosphere of romance. It should also be noted that with this episode and others like it, Meredith appears to be satisfying Dame Gossip's appetite for the "wonderful."

Despite Fleetwood's swashbuckling facade and his role as ostensible romantic hero of the novel, Carinthia proves to be more than a match for him in the contest of wills which comprises the substance of the book. But her triumph is not immediate, since Fleetwood's appearance succeeds in fooling her into believing that she has found someone who is worthy of her submission. Just after her marriage, for instance, we discover her feelings as she sits mutely beside her husband atop a racing coach:

> Her husband's mastery of the reins endowed him with the beauty of those harmonious trotters he guided and kept to their pace; and the humming rush of the pace, the smooth torrent of the brown heath-knolls and reddish pits and hedge-lines and grass-flats and copses pouring the counterway of her advance, belonged to his wizardry. The bearing of her onward was her abandonment to him. (p. 189)

One thing especially should be noted about this passage—Carinthia's affinity with movement, process, kinesis rather than stasis; we shall have occasion to refer to this attribute later. Similarly, Fleetwood has reasons for marrying Carinthia, which lead to his quick disenchantment soon after the marriage proper. From our first introduction to him, he strikes us as a man engaged in a holy quest. Before he ever meets Carinthia, he hears Gower Woodseer, the Vernon Whitford of this novel, describe her in glowing metaphors which seize him instantly. "You have done what I thought impossible—" he cries to Woodseer, "fused a woman's face and grand scenery, to make them inseparable." And then, in words that are greatly revealing, he asks: "Where is she now? I have no wish to find her, but I want thoroughly to believe in her." (pp. 99-100) Of course, no living woman could ever have met Fleetwood's aesthetic or spiritual requirements. He abandons her almost immediately after the marriage.

The middle sections of the novel gradually trace the frustrated descent of Fleetwood from a position of popular eminence to castoff husband. Simultaneously, Carinthia becomes the idol of the masses, who read of her redoubtable exploits in that Victorian equivalent of modern fan magazines, the ballads which emanate from the Seven Dials Press. These exploits are far too numerous to list here; but she does acquire the epithet of "Whitechapel Countess," at first in derision of her pursuit of Fleetwood through the streets of London, but later as a suitable description of her total independence and personal nobility. Ironically, and despite Dame Gossip's protestations that truly heroic living disappeared with the preceding generation, Carinthia Jane becomes a worthy successor to her wildly unconventional mother, the Countess Fanny. Near the end of the novel, she caps her activities by joining her brother Chillon as he leaves for Spain to fight for the Queen in the Carlist Wars. The defeated Fleetwood follows the advice of his friend Lord Feltre, a Roman Catholic nobleman, and enters a monastery where he eventually dies.

It is customary to explain the incompatibility of Fleetwood and Carinthia in terms of Meredith's many pronouncements on the dangers of egoism. Certainly this is a legitimate way of interpreting the novel, and yet Fleetwood is not just another Sir Willoughby or Austin Feverel. For one thing, Sir Willoughby exemplifies the egoist's need *to possess*, whereas Fleetwood's driving passion becomes the spiritual need *to be possessed*. As such, his monastic fate is inevitable. Carinthia, quite obviously, could never please a man whose requirements for a wife are that she be as much like the Madonna as possible. Indeed, she meets an antithetical set of requirements. She represents, in fact she embodies, that vitally active, inflexible, and enduring force for which we have no better name than, simply, Nature. "I hate sleep," Carinthia tells her brother early in the book; "I hate anything that robs me of my will." (p. 50) It becomes very clear, therefore, that Carinthia's inability to understand anything about the nature of gambling in Chapter IX stems from her complete trust in the powers of her own individual will. Any gambler must place some trust in Fortune, an act of submission which is inconceivable to Carinthia, who must carve out her own destiny in a manner which would be incomprehensible to Hardy's Tess.

Perhaps an illustration from the text will serve to make clearer what I believe to have been Meredith's purpose in the creation of Carinthia. Fleetwood first sees her in a moment of lyrical vision: she is perched precariously on a shoot of timber, and immediately he concludes that she is "a noble daughter of the woods" who "might really be taken to symbolize the forest life" (p. 152). The scene reminds us of similar moments of lyrical apprehension in *Richard Feverel*, with one important difference. Lucy Desborough remains the source of what Stephen Dedalus called "esthetic stasis," or the ideal contemplation of the beautiful. But much more is implicit in the forest scene of *The Amazing Marriage*, since it is alluded to directly after the marriage of Fleetwood and Carinthia in the following passage. Fleetwood offers his arm to assist Carinthia in mounting the coach.

> "No, my husband, I can do it," unaided, was implied.
>
> Her stride from the axle of the wheel to the step higher would have been a graceful spectacle on Alpine crags.
>
> Fleetwood swallowed that, too, though it conjured up a mocking recollection of the Baden woods, and an astonished wild donkey preparing himself for his harness. A sour relish of the irony in his present position sharpened him to devilish enjoyment of it, as the finest form of loathing: on the principle, that if we find ourselves consigned to the nether halls, we do well to dance drunkenly. He had cried for Romance—here it was! (pp. 185-86)

We witness here the translation of the earlier lyrical moment into an incident which establishes Carinthia's independent vitality and capacity for significant action or movement. At the same time the scene confirms the reversal of roles which I mentioned earlier. Carinthia begins to take on the aspect of a heroine of romance as her poetic function as a symbol of dynamic nature becomes clearer; Fleetwood becomes more and more the comic butt. Numerous instances of this movement in the novel could be cited.

Curiously, then, Fleetwood resembles Joyce's Dedalus in his stuffy, churchy disdain for the physical, the kinetic aspect of experience in his quest for ideal forms of beauty. Therefore, Meredith's defiance of Dame Gossip, with her preference for action and the evocation of wonder in a story, is not nearly as total as we might assume. Carinthia, as I see her, is a much larger portrait of Clara Middleton of *The Egoist*, whose will is most memorably manifest in the daring flight from Patterne Hall. With the character of Carinthia, Meredith uses that flight as the symbolic basis for a revised aesthetic of characterization in his fiction. Perhaps the best direct statement of that aesthetic appears in the following words of Gower Woodseer, which incidentally form an excellent theoretical rebuttal to the notions of Stephen Dedalus:

. . . People talk of perfect beauty: suitable for paintings and statues. Living faces, if they're to show the soul, which is the star on the peak of beauty, must lend themselves to commotion. Nature does it in a breezy tree or over ruffled waters. Repose has never such splendid reach as animation—I mean, in the living face. Artists prefer repose. Only Nature can express the uttermost beauty with her gathering and tuning of discords. Well, [Carinthia] has that beauty. I remember my impression when I saw her first on her mountains abroad. Other beautiful faces of women go pale, grow stale. The diversified in the harmony of the flash are Nature's own, her radiant, made of her many notes, beyond our dreams to reproduce. (p. 397)

Of course, Carinthia's function as a poetic device rather than as a realistic character may make too much of a demand on the reader's credibility. I think, however, we would be wise in agreeing with Professor Stevenson that *The Amazing Marriage* satisfied the same romantic impulse for Meredith as *The Tempest* did for Shakespeare.[21]

[1] "Spatial Form in Modern Literature," *Sewanee Review*, LIII (1945), pp. 221-40, 433-56; *The Golden Nightingale* (New York, 1949), ch. III; *Anatomy of Criticism* (Princeton, 1957); *The Philosophy of Literary Form* (New York, 1957), Vintage ed.

[2] *The Ordeal of Richard Feverel*, ed. Charles J. Hill (New York, 1964), Rinehart ed., p. 11. The text used in this reprint is that of the first edition. Hereafter, page numbers will follow quotations in the body of the text.

[3] *Dombey and Son* (London, 1960), Everyman ed., pp. 20-21.

[4] *An Age of Fiction, The Nineteenth Century British Novel* (New York, 1964), p. 225.

[5] *The Novel and the Modern World* (Chicago, 1960), pp. 152-53.

[6] *Art and Substance in George Meredith* (Lincoln, Nebr., 1953), p. 161.

[7] *The Ordeal of George Meredith* (New York, 1953), p. 66.

[8] "The Novels of George Meredith," in *The Common Reader*, Second Series (5th ed.; London, 1948), pp. 228-230.

[9] In a later version of the poem, Meredith changed line 6 from "Press her dreaming lips as her waist I folded slow" to "Press her parting lips as her waist I gather slow."

[10] *Granite and Rainbow* (New York, 1958), p. 138.

[11] *The Philosophy of Literary Form* (New York, 1957), pp. 26-27.

[12] *George Meredith* (New York, 1926), p. 145.

[13] John W. Morris, "Inherent Principles of Order in *Richard Feverel*," *PMLA*, LXXVIII (1963), p. 334.

[14] Quoted in Patricia Thomson's *The Victorian Heroine, A Changing Ideal 1837-1873* (London, 1956), p. 140.

[15] See Phyllis Bartlett's "Richard Feverel: Knight Errant," *Bulletin of the New York Public Library*, LXIII, pp. 329-40, for a thorough look at this aspect of the novel.

[16] Stevenson, *op. cit.*, p. 309.

[17] *The Amazing Marriage* (New York, 1930), p. 11. Page references will again directly follow the quotations.

[18] *Op. cit.*, p. 320.

[19] Norman Kelvin associates the Dame with Meredith's many other attempts to supply a choral voice in his narration; he sees her as "Meredith's final effort in his novels to give body and voice to society, though society is no longer the sophisticated sensibility it was in *The Egoist* or *The Essay on Comedy*." *A Troubled Eden* (Stanford, 1961), pp. 189-90.

[20] In "Meredith's Late Novels: Suggestions for a Critical Approach," *Nineteenth-Century Fiction*, XIX (1964), pp. 282 ff., Joseph Kruppa uses Professor Frye's distinctions in a brief but valuable discussion of the structure of *The Amazing Marriage*.

[21] *Op. cit.*, p. 322.

THOMAS D. CLARESON

Wilkie Collins to Charles Reade:
Some Unpublished Letters

WHILE ALL OF THEIR BIOGRAPHERS agree that Wilkie Collins and Charles Reade were close friends, Kenneth Robinson, echoing Malcolm Elwin, states the basic problem: "Although Reade announced his intention of preserving Wilkie's letters as heirlooms for his family, no such collection appears to have survived. Indeed little evidence remains of this significant friendship between two of the most popular writers of their time."[1]

Among the papers owned by Michael Reade, present Squire of Ipsden, are twenty-seven letters written by Wilkie Collins to Reade or Laura Seymour and dating between 4 June 1861 and 17 July 1883.[2] Despite certain letters in known collections, these, I believe, may be identified with the group to which Robinson refers, although what percentage of the total correspondence they represent one can only conjecture. Obviously they do not make up its entirety—not only because of the letters already known (almost all of which are from Reade to Collins),[3] but also because the *Memoir of Charles Reade* (1887) quotes from letters that do not exist among the twenty-seven, and finally, because the letters themselves refer to still others.

All of their biographers agree that by the time of the *Griffith Gaunt* episode of 1867, when Collins defended Reade against charges of indecency, the men were becoming close friends. Nuel Pharr Davis, however, suggests that Reade was "probably" one of the guests at the luncheon given by Collins for Millais when the latter went north to marry the former Mrs. Ruskin in 1855,[4] while

Robinson considers them "little more than acquaintances" at the time Collins's *No Name* was published in December 1862 and finds the "first evidence of a growing friendship" in 1867.[5] The earliest of the new letters, written from 12, Harley Street, 4 June, 1861, seems to argue Robinson more nearly correct, though somewhat late. It salutes "My dear Reade":

> I am sincerely glad to hear that you have got some rest and change. You have the work of a writer to do in this world, as well as the work of a reformer—and you have earned (and more than earned) the right to turn your back on the annoyances, delays, and disappointments of litigation, and to take breath again in a higher and purer atmosphere both for body and mind.

Fortunately, this replies directly to one of the letters from Reade to Collins in the Parrish Collection at Princeton and thus permits its exact dating for the first time. On 31 May [1861], writing from Margate, Charles had "promised myself every day the pleasure of calling upon you; but unfortunately postponed it until I was so ill that I had to leave town and come here. My complaint was relaxed uvula brought on I believe by the worry and anxiety of Reade v. this thief and Reade v. that rogue and Reade v the other swindler." He then hoped that Wilkie was "better employed, and preparing another great success," asserted that Margate was far superior to the "shipless sea" of Brighton, and reported that Frank Robson was recuperating there at Margate.[6]

Point by point Wilkie answers him: "I entirely agree with you about the shipless sea at Brighton. My usual sea-side resort of late years has been Broadstairs. . . . I like Margate too"; "as for my present proceedings, I am slowly putting up the scaffolding of the book which is yet to be built [*No Name*]"; and "Give my kindest regards to Robson." He concludes:

> Except short trips of a day or two, I shall be in town (probably) till the end of July—If you are ever near here, between this time and that, come and 'report yourself' to yours very truly Wilkie Collins.

The language, especially with regard to the proposed social calls, and the meticulousness with which Wilkie replies to every topic suggest the formality between acquaintances, particularly when compared with later letters. The best evidence occurs, however, when Wilkie anticipates that he will probably be at Broadstairs during the autumn:

> ... alternating hard work at a new story, with short trips to sea in the roomy old English luggers of my friends and allies the boatmen. If you could come on one of those trips, we might make a pleasant time of it. I assume—after "Love Me Little, Love Me Long" (Vol 2nd)—that you and the sea understand each other thoroughly, and never disagree under any circumstances however stormy!

That this is an assumption speaks for itself; moreover, whatever be the legends of Newhaven, a letter by Charles's brother, Edward Anderdon, addressed from Paris to his wife, 25 August 1856, includes as part of a description of the Channel crossing:

> I found Charles at the Folkestone station, and we went in his same carriage to Dover and were in time for the packet. It was however rather windy, and Charles, who is easily seasick, lay down in his cabin.[7]

Certainly the two letters establish the beginning of their friendship not later than the summer of 1861, though not necessarily having its inception then. The letters imply, too, that the acquaintance existed primarily, if not solely, in correspondence, though both men seemed eager for a meeting.

After a lapse of five years the tone of the second and third letters from Collins, both dated in July 1866 from Welcombe Place, has changed. Without doubt both letters refer to his unsuccessful dramatization of *Armadale* and imply that he consulted Reade perhaps even before he consulted Dickens. On July 3 he seeks practical advice:

> The gout (which upsets my head as well as my foot) bothered me so when I was with you today, that I forgot one of the things I had to ask you. I think I told you that the terms I suggested to Mr. Coleman were to be terms 'by the night'. But we came to no conclusion about what they were to be—and he

is to come to me on Friday or Saturday to settle this, if he is in town. I have mislaid your letter telling me what ought to be done under these circumstances. But, (since I came home) inspired by *Potash*, I have recovered memory enough to remember that you said either £1.10 or £2– a night. Will you, like a good fellow, tell me which sum I ought to stipulate for? It is needless to add that I shall of course not refer to you in this matter when I make the arrangement with Mr. Coleman. I only want to know what I ought to ask.

On July 9 attention turns to the play itself:

> I send you my play by book-post today. You will see one 'cut' suggested in Act I—and I shall bring Act III closer here and there. Remember this when you read it—and tell me what you think my chance if I get on the stage. Also, give me any suggestions which occur to you—who look at the piece with a fresh eye.

So emerges, as might be expected, one of the dominant topics of the entire group of letters: Wilkie's deliberate seeking—and giving —of advice with regard to literary matters, especially in reference to drama, though not exclusively so. The other two major topics are an ever-increasing concern for his own and Reade's health and an ever-growing social intimacy. Indeed, five of the letters may assume somewhat secondary importance, perhaps, because they are little more than notes extending or declining invitations.[8] Two of the letters locate Collins in Paris, on 18 October 1876 and 4 December 1877, the second time explicitly with Caroline Graves. On 20 November 1871 "The two Carolines send you their love, and join in asking you not to forget no. 90." Were no other evidence whatsoever available, this letter in itself would establish the date by which Mrs. Graves returned to 90 Gloucester Place after her sojourn as the wife of Joseph Clow, the plumber. Throughout the letters the most conspicuous absence is the lack of any reference whatsoever to Martha Rudd (Mrs. Watson), the mother of Wilkie's three children.

A sub-group of nine letters, the first dated 22 September 1869, directly address Mrs. Laura Seymour, the actress and Reade's companion for more than twenty years. In that first letter Collins is "delighted to hear that you like the beginning of the story—the beginning is half the battle. I have just finished the weekly part to be published at the end of *February*—so I have a pretty good start at the printers thus far. May you like it as it goes on, as well as you like it now." This must be *Man and Wife*, serialized in *Cassell's* between January and September 1870. On 22 September 1871 he is pleased "to find that my young friend 'Miss Finch' has produced such a strongly favorable impression on you. I hope you will find the Story does not drop as it goes on. My great guns are still in reserve." On 24 October 1874 in response to her praise of what must be *The Law and the Lady*, published in February 1875, he assures her: "My proof-book is entirely at your service—if you would like to read what is completed of the story. I have written to Mrs. Lehmann, who is now reading it, to send it on to you as soon as she has done." And on 19 April 1876, Laura Seymour becomes "the trump of trumps—and the best and truest of friends" for her praise of *Miss Gwilt*, just opened the night before at the Globe theatre. She seems to have become as much of an Egeria for Collins as she was for Reade.

This same letter holds further interest because it reveals the emotional state of Collins on an opening night:

> I have but one excuse for not having sent you the best places in the theatre—I was *afraid* to ask any of my friends to go to the first night. Though I had but one eye to look through, on the few last occasions when I could go to rehearsal, I saw that the scenery was so backward and (excepting the first act) so bad, and the people connected with this theatre (for the most part) such a set of incapable idiots and blackguards—that I fully anticipated a failure on the first night—and I own I did not like the idea of inviting my friends to hear me hissed! The kindness of the audience, as things really were (I believe they caught it mesmerically from *you*) has really left me deeply grateful. Never before have I been so indebted to my good and dear public.
>
> At 8 o'clock the scenes were not all ready! At 9 o'clock the scoundrels of carpenters were lying about *drunk*—and their chief utterly lost his head. No more of it! I have not been able to prevail upon myself to go near the theatre since.

Returning to Mrs. Seymour, during the 1870's when Caroline Graves apparently became as close a friend to her and Reade as had Wilkie, the letters take on a fresh intimacy, though none surviving was written by Mrs. Graves. One, dated 30 December 1875, shows well the increasingly informal tone:

My dear Mrs. Seymour,

I had hoped to be able to call today and thank you for the delicious prawn. But the horrid necessity of "keeping in advance of the printer's" chains me to my desk—so my gratitude must exhale itself on paper. When I say that I don't go to bed without a bit of the prawn to keep me company, you will understand that your present is appreciated as it ought to be.

In a little while I hope to have some proofs for you to read. Meanwhile, Caroline sends you some German cake which has just arrived from Berlin—and begs you to accept it. I had asked her to go and see how Reade was (not being able to go myself) —and so she was unfortunately out when you called.

My love to Reade

Yrs affly
WC

To this gourmet's exhalation he adds the excited note: "We had great luck with the Dramatic 'Armadale' at Liverpool. The audience received the piece with open arms. It never was in jeopardy for a moment."

In like manner, in the only letter known to survive between Charles and Mrs. Graves, dated 18 November [1878], during Mrs. Seymour's final illness, Reade writes:

2 Albert Terrace
Knightsbridge
18 November

Dear Mrs. Graves,

I cannot thank you enough for your kindness in bringing me [*sic*] us this fine old whiskey. It has been my right arm in dealing with poor dear Seymour. She is so weakened by pain that she needs an occasional stimulant, and this is literaly [*sic*] the only one that does not assist the gout but rather counteracts it.

She had yesterday a longer intermission of pain than usual but we have had so many ups and downs I am afraid to be too sanguine. Once more thank you for your kindness and judgment.

Yours trly,
Charles Reade[9]

Perhaps the most intriguing letters from Collins to Mrs. Seymour, however, are those disclosing her activities in regard to several of his plays. A letter dated 16 April 1873 indicates that she seriously considered a role in *The New Magdalen*, which opened at the Olympic on May 19, but complained because the role lost significance in Act III. "If we had time to talk this matter over," Wilkie replies, "something might be done—but we have *no* time." He continues:

> I am in danger of losing my copyright if this piece is produced first in America. I *must produce* a representative of Lady Janet on the Roll Coupons at rehearsal.
>
> Under these circumstances, I am forced to decide *at once*. I have no alternative.
>
> Let me therefore thank you most sincerely for your kind readiness to consider the part, and say frankly that I place it in other hands because *I* see, as *you* see, that it does not give you the opportunities which it ought to offer in the last act of the piece. With renewed thanks believe me most truly yours Wilkie Collins.

Her failure to play Lady Janet may, in part at least, explain why she took the managership of the Queens Theatre for the 1873-1874 season. Reade's *The Wandering Heir* opened there November 22, and the season ran until 4 July 1874. After this last venture as a London manager, Mrs. Seymour seems to have been contented as Egeria to Collins's efforts of 1876 and 1877. As for him, although this letter reveals the only anger toward Reade or Mrs. Seymour in any of the letters, it anticipates his tirades to them both against Henry Neville, manager of the Olympic, who revived Collins and Dickens's *No Thoroughfare* in November 1876.[10] At the end of a letter dated 10 November 1876, in which he blames Neville for his own absence from "today's full rehearsal," he thanks Mrs. Seymour "for all that your kindness has done for the piece."

Most important, she was closely connected with the production of *The Moonstone*, which finally opened at the Olympic 17 September 1877, after having been rejected the year before by the Bancrofts.[11] It failed, having but a short run. On 25 May 1877 Collins writes:

My dear Mrs Seymour,

I have no wish to introduce 'a firebrand' into the theatre— and we will certainly *try* all that can be done to find another actor as good as Mr. Firebrand [Original name scratched out.] without personal directions to him. The misfortune is that I am still crippled by my rheumatic knees—when I ought to be going to the theatres and looking out for the men that the piece wants. Milder weather is my only hope because it will allow me to get out.

>*Betteredge*
>*Gooky Ablewhite*
>*Sargeant Cuff*

How are we to cast those three parts? I write to Mr. Neville today to ask him what he thinks about engaging *Mr. Mead*— whose 'Pistol' in Henry the Fifth struck me as showing him to be a thoroughly trustworthy actor.

>Yrs affly
>WC

On 4 July 1877, "In great haste":

My dear Mrs Seymour

Caroline left at your house yesterday the first act of *The Moonstone.*

The second act I am now correcting for you. You have only to send me a line when you want it.

I should have written yesterday—but I was very busy with Neville on the subject of the 'cast.' We have decided this difficult question to my entire satisfaction. If the negotiations proceed, the complete performance will, as I believe, be really remarkable.

I hear you go to Margate this afternoon. May the weather be all that you can wish! and may Miss Clack begin to assume a living form when you return! (N.B. I am quite confident about

Miss Clack and the public with *you* to make them known to each other).

Yrs affly

WC

My love to Reade

Finally, on 13 September [1877]:

My dear Mrs. Seymour,

My knees won't work today—they are so rheumatic that I cannot attend this rehearsal. Rest will soon put me right again.

The plaid which you so kindly lent to me is in Alfred's care.

Yours ever

WC

When *The Moonstone* opened September 17, Mrs. Seymour played the role of Miss Clack.[12] It was her last stage appearance, for that autumn her terminal illness, cancer of the liver, grew active. By December 4 Wilkie and Caroline sent their sincerest sympathy to her from Paris, having just learned of her illness when they returned from Italy. Upon the occasion of her death, Wilkie writes to Charles on 29 September 1879:

With all my heart, I will be with you tomorrow. You know how I appreciated her fine qualities as an artist, and how sincerely I admired and prized her bright true and generous nature as a woman. In some degree at least, my dear old friend, I may claim to share in your sorrow, and to value as I ought the sad privilege of paying the last tribute of affection and respect to her memory.

Yours affectionately,

Wilkie Collins.

I will take care to be at your house, punctually to the time—11.30.

As for the main body of letters to Reade himself, they continue the three dominant topics: literary matters, social engagements, and personal health. A letter of 19 November 1871 proves that Reade supplied Collins with documenatary materials: "I ought to have thanked you long ago for so kindly sending me these abstracts. They are most interesting and I shall certainly use them in 'Poor Miss F.' " In the

[115]

same letter he offers to introduce Reade to an agent so as to produce the dramatization of *Griffith Gaunt* in the U.S., if arrangements have not already been made. The very next day, November 20, he reports that the dramatization of *The Woman in White*—referred to as "the 'business' "—"promises famously. Receipts of the first week £475—which gives a good profit to those interested, at starting. This weeks returns, steadily larger every day than last weeks." After assuring Charles that a private box awaits him, especially early in the week, Wilkie reminds him:

> A new stock of *Moselle* is at this moment being put into the cellar. Come and draw a cork between 3 & 4, as soon as you get to town—or at 7.30, when there is dinner.
> The two Carolines send you their love, and join in asking you not to forget No. 90. I am all in arrear with 'Poor Miss F.'—in consequence of these dramatic doings. You don't say a word about your play. Another reason for tasting the Moselle. I want to hear about it.

Although perhaps peripheral to our central interest, on 2 February 1876, added to a purely social note, he comments: "Another old friend gone—in Forster! He was angry with me because I did not 'consult him' before I went to America! I am glad to think now I was never angry with *him*." On 18 October 1876 from Hotel Westminster, Paris, he delivers his tirade against Neville for "casting [*No Thoroughfare*] without allowing me a voice in the matter.... I shall not attend the rehearsals" because of Neville's action "and because I have not the slightest hope of doing anything to any good purpose with some of the actors engaged—notably with Mrs. Stirling." On 21 March 1879 when he sends Reade and Mrs. Seymour, both ill, a copy of *The Fallen Leaves* to read, he scrawls across the top of the page: "Try some good wine—and beware of whiskey and water (the last fashionable delusion of the doctors!)"

Fortunately Collins's letter of 21 March 1876 directly replies to another of the Reade letters in the Parrish Collection; it is the often-partially-quoted one of which Nuel Pharr Davis asserts, "Moved by [its] affectionately insincere assurances," Wilkie dedicated *The Two Destinies* to Charles.[13] This evaluation must be modified, I believe, in light of Collins's letter written within two days of his receipt of Charles's.

> Just a word (by means of Miss Graves's pen) to thank you heartily for your friendly and consoling letter. You know what a very high value I set on your opinion in questions of Art, and you will not be surprised to hear that you have encouraged me just at a time when I wanted such encouragement as only a brother writer can give.
>
> I am beginning to hope that I have passed through the worst and fiercest ordeal of the pain, and that the disease will be content this time with attacking one eye only. In the inevitable absence of poor Beard still laid up, I am looked after by Mr. Critchett, who is not only a great occulist [*sic*], but also the kindest and pleasantest of men.
>
> Thank Mrs. Seymour for her kind words, and with my love to you both,
>
> Always yours.—
Wilkie Collins

This is the only letter in the entire group in the hand of his amanuensis, Mrs. Graves's daughter. Certainly Charles's letter must be read in light of Wilkie's severe illness and attendant depression.

> Dear Collins,
>
> I am truly sorry to hear you are suffering from gout in the eye again.
>
> This is the cause of all your troubles being so painful and so hard on you in your art. I do hope you will soon recover, and resume those labors, which to my mind were never more successful.
>
> In this story, Temple bar, [*sic*] as far as I have read it, there is a pace of language, and a vein of sweet tenderness rising through the work, which reveal maturing genius.
>
> It is deplorable that such an artist as you now reaching your zenith should carry such heavy weight in every race you run with your contemporaries.
>
> You can distance them all the same: but I who know and value you in private as well as in public do deeply deplore the distress

and pain in which you have to write these works that afford un-
mixed pleasure to others.

I hope to hear better accts and believe me [man . . .]
Yrs very sincerly [*sic*]
Charles Reade

Mrs. Seymour sends her kind love and sympathy.[14]

The tone of both letters resumes the formality of the earliest letters, and both men give their full signatures, for whatever these details may be worth. If to say such things to a long-standing intimate is
"affectionately insincere," then Reade is guilty; if not, he is most con-
siderate.

Of all the letters the most extensive and the one best showing the
degree to which each wanted to help the other in literary matters was
written by Collins on "Thursday May 29 [1871] (In bed)" after the
opening night of *Free Labour*, the dramatic adaptation of *Put Yourself in His Place*, staged at the Adelphi:

> I tried to get to you last night—but I had no idea where you
> were, and could not find out—until you bowed from a Private
> Box. And *then* I could not get upstairs in time to meet you.
> My verdict is that the immense difficulties of dramatizing the
> story have been met and conquered in a most masterly way—
> and that the play contains some of the most interesting and the
> most original scenes that I have beheld for many a long year
> past. The acting decidedly good. Neville—Grotait—the work-
> men (those silent as well as those speaking) all excellent. Of
> the ladies, Miss Erskine best—judged by last night's ordeal. She
> was well *in* her part, and has unquestionable ability. Miss
> Young—personally (to me) much the most interesting woman
> of the two, appeared to be over-weighted. But I *thought* she was
> terribly frightened—and I wait to see her again. At present, she
> strikes me as a charming actress in sentimental comedy—called
> upon a little too suddenly to rise to the expression of strong
> emotion in strong drama.
> Now as to making the piece popular—in other words as to
> cutting out. Here are my views (right or wrong) *Act I*
> Shifty Dick, on his entrance, does'nt [*sic*] express himself to
> those who have not read the story. Who is he? Why does he

come on, disguised as a Frenchman? *I* should take the scene out, and bring him in later—after he has been talked about so that *the audience may recognize him when he appears.*

Act II

The old church. Admirable scene. *Less* forging—it is excellently done—but you destroy the effect of making the knife, by the previous hammering & beating. *No ghosts—no marriage vision*—the people don't understand it. Don't let Neville speak when the door is being taken off its hinges—he *prevents the audience from seeing the door disappear*—Let him look at the door—say "Did I hear something *out*side?" and wait, looking at the door. *Then* the people will look at the door—and that admirable scene will be heightened. N.B. Mr Ashley must not wear a chimney pot hat on a country excursion—don't let him try to look as if he had been snowed on. 'Suppose' the snow, unless you can be *sure* of having it well done.

Act IV

Don't let Shifty Dick stand waiting to be caught. Out with his marriage speech—don't let him appear until Neville has come on, and Ashley has taunted him. Then let Shifty Dick be brought on to be identified by living evidence as well as photographic evidence—in his clergyman's clothes—supposed to have been arrested as he was leaving the vestry to join the wedding party. 'Is this Shifty Dick?'—'Yes!'—'Is *that* the man who married them?'—'Yes!"—Hooray! and on with the handcuffs.

Act III

I find myself with less vivid recollections of this act than of the others. An excellent scene with Grotait and the fulminating box is before me vividly—and the blown-up mill I remember. But no more. Are there bits that might come out here? I suspect there are.

Mr. Cheatham must be made to *speak up.* Down with that damned 'Prompter's Box' advertisement over the door—and up with the old church, and the fight, in its place.
Advertise more largely in Times and Daily Telegraph and Standard.

I see no advertisement in the Echo—an immense circulation. Rectify this.

A big Poster of the old church on all the prominent boardings.

———

All these things I would have called and *said*—but my miserable book *won't* get finished. I must stay at home and work. So I send Mrs. Graves with this. Between 3 and 4. if you are this way, you will find me. After 4 I go out—and then dine at Highgate. Lehmann has come back.

Once more, I congratulate you on this piece. All depends now on judicious cutting and judicious management. If there is anything I can do, command me.

Yrs ever
WC

Let this letter stand emblematic of their intimacy: it contains it all, even the social invitation and Mrs. Graves as courier. Here are revealed two men—Collins with his sense of the dramatic and of story, Reade with his flair for theatricality and for an elaborate attempt at realism—helping to make a friend's work stronger, more effective. Prompt books in the hands of the Reade family indicate that Reade tried to follow Wilkie's advice.

In sharp contrast stands the last of the surviving letters. Dated 17 July 1883, it reads:

My dear Reade,

In clearing out a drawer filled with old letters, my hair has stood on end at the discovery of a letter of mine (addressed to *you*)—shuffled up with the other papers. It was a reply to a kind letter of yours telling me of your illness and asking me if I could recommend any good modern novels that you might find worth reading. How I could have missed my own letter with the others the devil, who must have possessed me, only knows. But what must *you* have thought of your old friend? I can only remember that you are the kindest of men, and that you will excuse the frail fellow creature who signs himself yours always truly

Wilkie Collins

You have lost nothing by the loss of the letter. It only acknowledged *my* inability to read any *new* novels—and referred you facetiously to the *old* novels that you know already.

There speaks a man whose literary era has ended—a man who, like Reade, produced if not the finest, at least some of the most memorable Victorian fiction.

These letters have their ultimate value in confirming without doubt the intimacy of Reade and Collins. Various inferences may be drawn, but at this time I should like to leave them unverbalized—except for one. Walter de la Mare once speculated casually that Reade may have shown Collins the jewel which became *The Moonstone.*[15]

In the possession of Michael Reade's sister Winwood is a "Moonstone pendant made from a single moonstone of flattened circular shape, approximately 3 cm. in diameter and 1½ cm. thick, and weighing approximately 100 cts., mounted in a fairly light, but attractive silver cage."[16]

Charles's older brother, Edward Anderdon, was long a member of the Indian Civil Service. Last man into Agra during the Sepoy Mutiny of 1857, he actually assumed command of that post when its commander collapsed, apparently in nervous fatigue. By 1860 he had returned to England, and in subsequent years may well have met Wilkie, who, of course, had written about the Mutiny. This last is highly conjectural, and is not actually necessary. In a series of letters from India during 1856-1857 to his wife when she was dying at Brighton, Edward writes on 21 September 1856:

> I bought a whole handful of specimens for a couple of Rupees from which after selecting and testing by the Benares jeweler, I shall send you the best. You have not I think a cairngorum [*sic*] amongst your collection, and one specimen is a very fine one, but I could get no moonstones for Charles.

Even more important is an undated letter directly to Charles from India; reference to his litigation with Bentley and other internal evidence, however, do place it early in the 1857-1858 period. Edward writes:

> You must prize that moonstone. They are not now to be had of that size for any money, and the person from whom I got it

some years ago offered to give me 15£ for it if I restored it. I have a decent cairngorum [*sic*] added to my collection but in the march of 800 miles I have got only one small chalcedony and this we purchased up on the road, in a repass, where no such formation can exist. It must have been dropped by some traveller.17

There can be little doubt that this is the stone now in the possession of Winwood Reade. Whether or not Collins ever met Edward Anderdon, certainly such a jewel and stories of a renowned individual who commanded a post during the Mutiny may have influenced Wilkie's imagination. This conjecture, of course, in no way eliminates the many other influences working upon Collins. Far from it; yet he did not entitle the novel *The Kohinoor Diamond*. It is *The Moonstone*.

[1] Kenneth Robinson, *Wilkie Collins: A Biography* (New York, 1951), p. 279.

[2] These letters are owned by Michael Reade, who has graciously lent them to me. A chronological listing of the letters is as follows:

4 June 1861 (Reply Reade 31 May), 6 pp.
3 July 1866, 4 pp.
9 July 1866, 2 pp.
22 November 1869 (Seymour), 2 pp.
29 May 1871, 3 pp. (oversize)
22 September 1871 (Seymour), 3 pp.
19 November 1871, 4 pp.
20 November 1871, 4 pp.
4 December 1872, 3 pp.
16 April 1873 (Seymour), 3 pp.
24 October 1874 (Seymour), 3 pp.
30 December 1875 (Seymour), 3 pp.
2 February 1876, 2 pp.
21 March 1876 (Reply Reade 19 March), 3 pp.
19 April 1876 (Seymour), 5 pp.
18 October 1876, 4 pp.
10 November 1876 (Seymour), 3 pp.
29 December 1876, 3 pp.
25 May 1877 (Seymour), 3 pp.
4 July 1877 (Seymour), 3 pp.

13 September [1877], 1 p.
4 December 1877, 1 p.
14 July 1878, 2 pp.
21 March 1879, 1 p.
29 September 1879, 3 pp.
17 July 1883, 3 pp.
14 May [?], 1 p.
In reproducing the texts of the letters, I have retained Collin's idiosyncrasies of spelling, punctuation, etc., to preserve accuracy of text.

[3] The McIntosh MSS, cited by Nuel Pharr Davis, contain no letters between Collins and Reade. The Sercombe-Smith MSS, also cited, are at this time unavailable in the hands of a private collector. Davis, however, quotes only one letter from Collins to Reade, and that an invitation to dinner on 29 August 1871. Nuel Pharr Davis, *The Life of Wilkie Collins* (Urbana, 1956), pp. 267-68.

[4] Davis, pp. 175-76.

[5] Robinson, pp. 169, 200.

[6] Four pp. A.L.S., quoted by permission of the Princeton University Library.

[7] This letter is owned by Lt. Col. A. H. N. Reade, who has graciously lent it to me.

[8] 4 December 1872, Wilkie cannot make a dinner engagement.
2 February 1876, Wilkie cannot make a dinner engagement.
29 December 1876, Wilkie declines dinner because of health.
14 July 1878, Wilkie had hoped to invite them to dinner, but cannot because of his health.
14 May [?], Wilkie invites them to luncheon.

[9] Two pp. A.L.S., reprinted by permission of the Pierpont Morgan Library. There are several reasons for dating this letter 1878. Not only were Wilkie and Caroline on the Continent late in the autumn of 1877 after the two-month run of *The Moonstone*, but Reade's remarks suggest Seymour has been ill for some time. Her terminal illness, as noted, became active in autumn of 1877, and she died 19 September 1879. An earlier date does not seem feasible because of the evidence of the earlier letters.

[10] Charles Eyre Pascoe, *The Dramatic List: The Principal Performances of Living Actors and Actresses of the British Stage* (London, 1879), pp. 251-52.

[11] Robinson, p. 286.

[12] Playbills from the Enthoven Collection, Victoria and Albert Museum, indicate that she opened in the role; however, by November 17, billed as the last performance of the play, she had been replaced by a Miss Gerard. While *The Moonstone* seems to have been quietly received by most jour-

nals, *The Illustrated Sporting and Dramatic News* (27 October 1877), under the heading "Our Captious Critic," is unfavorable and singles out Mrs. Seymour for her "ultra-farcical interpretation of the part."

[13] Davis, p. 283; also Robinson, pp. 277-78.

[14] Two pp. A.L.S., reprinted by permission of the Princeton University Library.

[15] Walter de la Mare, "The Early Novels of Wilkie Collins," in John Drinkwater, ed., *The Eighteen-Sixties* (New York, 1932), pp. 76-77 n.

[16] This description of the stone was prepared by H. Knowles-Brown Ltd., 27 Hampstead High Street, N.W. 3, in January 1962.

[17] Both letters are owned by Lt. Col. A. H. N. Reade and are now in my possession.

Index to the Essays